UNDER COLLEGE TOWERS

THE MACMILLAN COMPANY
NEW YORK · BOSTON · CHICAGO · DALLAS
ATLANTA · SAN FRANCISCO

MACMILLAN & CO., LIMITED
LONDON · BOMBAY · CALCUTTA
MELBOURNE

THE MACMILLAN CO. OF CANADA, LTD.
TORONTO

UNDER COLLEGE TOWERS

A Book of Essays

By
MICHAEL EARLS, S. J.

NEW YORK
THE MACMILLAN COMPANY
1926

All rights reserved

Copyright, 1926,
By THE MACMILLAN COMPANY.

Set up and electrotyped.
Published November, 1926.

Printed in the United States of America by
THE FERRIS PRINTING COMPANY, NEW YORK.

In Memoriam

Louise Imogen Guiney
Joyce Kilmer
Maurice Francis Egan

Tuis enim fidelibus, Domine, vita mutatur, non tollitur, et dissoluta terrestris hujus incolatus domo, aeterna in caelis habitatio comparatur.
Praefatio in Missis Defunctorum

CONTENTS

	PAGE
OCTOBER'S PALIMPSESTS	11
COLUMNISTS	19
POET'S POETS	38
LITERARY VAUDEVILLIANS	48
GAS-HOUSE POETRY	58
THE GENEARCHS OF LOUISE IMOGEN GUINEY	68
A MODERN STYLITES	88
FATHER SHEALY	100
THE SERVICE OF THE VOICE	123
A CLERIC'S LITERARY LABORATORIES	134

UNDER COLLEGE TOWERS

OCTOBER PALIMPSESTS

September is, in a very special sense, the true end of the year; not chronologically, as in the last days of December when dwarfed hours in shivering minutes crawl toward a new grave of time; not in dial evidences, as in a week when the sun-shadow is like the leprechaun, gone as soon as you take your eyes from that elusive fairy and his crock of gold; not ecclesiastically, for then it is Trinity Sunday, when faith lingers delightedly on a consoling prospect, such as Newman presents in the peroration of his sermon on that Feast. September rather is the beautiful valediction to the green world of nature, field and forest—excepting, of course, the perennial firs and pines, like nuns of the cloister, as Maria Chapdelaine saw them, "brave women of bitter wisdom," who abide in unchanging garb the year round: the trees, catholic on the landscape of all seasons; the nuns, Catholic in all the virtues of their vows.

September, therefore, writes *Finis* to nature's book of life for the year. The volume enlarges no more; it is placed away on the shelf—the grasses and weeds to bring out the new duodecimos in the spring, the shrubs and trees to resume their texts where they left off, like a man of character who possesses his soul in patience during a season of adversity, and in opportune time moves on in the full ardor of his vocation.

The book, however, is not bound in rigid clasps; for October, like a brown-garbed monk in a medieval *scriptorium*, comes gently in "on sandaled shoon" and (please find no winking pun here) turns over many an old leaf. His palette is rich enough with three only of the rainbow's colors— yellow, orange and red. At the other side of green, which is the pivotal heart of the seven prismatic colors, are blue, indigo and violet; but these are better suited to the soft spring days and the upper regions of the April skies. *Omne trinum perfectum:* and scholastic October is amply content with his threefold portion of the rainbow, harmonizing the innumerable tones, the semi-tones and decimiquavers.

With exquisite skill the autumnal ascetic achieves the splendid technique of textual illumination. The oaks and maples are his favorite manuscripts, capital letters, as it were, in high relief. Yet for the smaller texts, the *minuscula*, he displays a deft and delicate artistry. Consider the grasses of the field;

a rainbow in all its glory seems to be interlined with the meadows, and fragments of it are uncials of loveliness along the marshlands near the sea.

Alas! Unthinking tourists speed over mountain trails with hurried exclamations to scan the great quarto pages of the autumn book; but worthy sight-seers in true delight pause contemplatively before the iridescent footnotes in the humble margins. On a scroll of ordinary weeds, the architectonic spiders design the silver plaque of gossamer, worthy of the text of Solomon's Canticle. The famous Book of Kells, that marvelous witness to artistic skill—angelical it has been called—and witness also to the devout love of sacred texts in an old Gaelic monastery, may have its counterpart in any chapter of a stone wall or fence, enmeshed in vines and steeped in reedy growths along a country road.

The vine is a veritable scriptural whose interlinear readings are rich in clusters of purpling grapes. And if you observe a garden near-by, whose acre of golden wheat was gathered in midsummer, you may have an inquisitive meditation: which sheaf of wheat, which cluster of grapes may be called to the benediction of vocation, selected for the bread and wine at the altar. Other fields of higher import are rich for the harvest, said One whose voice still sounds appealingly: "pray ye the Lord of the harvest that he send forth laborers unto his harvest." And your meditation will continue, as you pass the school children on the road, wondering which of them will hearken to the Call, who to the cloister, who to the altar.

Yet it is not only through monastic windows that the glorious evidence of autumn's handicraft may be observed. There are pages of report for the ledgers of the man of the street in this final chapter of the year: gossip, too, for the social registers of the various Four Hundreds, those light cavalries of plutocratic society. September is for them, as for a great part of the animal world, the season of migrations. Trunks are packed and moved to another unabiding mansion, sometimes only twenty miles away, as from the Jersey coast to the high trees in Lakewood, or from the Maine headlands to the White Mountains. And great officials, who have important work to do, will have a longer route, let us say, from the Adirondacks to Washington.

Animals, too, are all a-foot and a-wing to winter quarters, some of them to burrow in subways near their summer tenements, others to revel in the coatless climes of Florida and lower California. The robins, for instance, those common minstrels who were busy and noisy on the lush lawns of April, foregathered in the September silence and have moved south fifteen blocks in latitude; their October address is Green Latitudes, 30°, 28', 17". The other common denizens of our region, the swallows, have removed their escadrilles from our skies; and their kindred companies, the martins, have already selected their castles in Southern climes. What praise has documented the hygienic and scenic selections of these feathery migrations; how they fascinated the eye of Shakespeare, that royal eye with which he endows the sight of Duncan when the king visits Macbeth at Dunsinane! Says Duncan:

> This castle hath a pleasant seat; the air
> Nimbly and sweely recommends itself
> Unto our gentle senses.

And Banquo, who knows our bevies of martins, though his printer calls them martlets, cites them as authorities on salubrious air:

> The guest of summer.
> The temple-haunting martlet, does approve,
> By his loved mansionry, that the heavens' breath
> Smells wooingly here; no jutty, frieze,
> Buttress, nor coign of vantage, but this bird
> Hath made his pendant bed and procreant cradle;
> Where they most breed and haunt, I have observed
> The air is delicate.

Yet October affords board and bed for such bird families as dare to brave the autumn and even the winter in our latitudes—the rowdy-dowdies of rough temperatures, the starlings, for instance, and those more ubiquitous commoners, the sparrows. The starlings, though versed in noisy chatter, have also a manual of exquisite songs, sweet little efforts of melody, though brief as punctuation points— commas and semi-colons. And Saint Augustine observed their ways of habitat to illustrate a sociological point in his "City of God": fifteen hundred years ago, hearing these choristers in Hippo, the great Doctor wrote, "now the starlings are of the gregarious kind." Five hundred years earlier the sparrows were pointed out for a higher lesson by the Supreme Teacher: "Are not five sparrows sold for two farthings, and not one of them is forgotten before God? . . . Fear not therefore; you are of more value than many sparrows."

What granaries are stored up by autumn for these little artisans during the winter months! Let the wintry flakes cover the land; these abecedarians in economics will know how to shake down a sufficient breakfast from the low reed pods or the high catalpa baskets upon the snow's white table-cloth. And if a bumptious scientist—the manneristic sciolist whose conclusions are far wider and less deep than his premises—possessed a mind for curative meditation he would become more than a scientist; certainly he would draw in the horns of theories that are butting against facts; he might even develop a philosopher, if not a poet. Else he must hear the sarcastic cachinnation of a buzzing wasp when he sees it in October making provision against the winter—the ingenuity of instinct, which, as in the case of the sphex, knows how to paralyze, and not kill, a caterpillar, so that its eggs may have living animal matter when they hatch. Now this mother wasp goes off and dies before the eggs develop; yet the offspring shall have the same ingenuity next year, and carry on the unchanging tradition to the end of the world. And if the microscopic scientist—we mean, of course, the sciolist—prates about evolution, he should hear the stinging laughter of Madame Sphex: "Buzz, buzz! My ancestors had this selfsame skill on the banks of the Nile six thousand years ago, and we do the job no better than they."

The sage and the saint, however, are adept readers of October's palimpsest. Poets who have not the catholic (not necessarily Catholic) vision often mistake the reading. Seeing only the surfaces of mutability, the flux of changing things, they may breathe in the sad melancholy of the old Greek stoics, who were sore of heart because of the wear-away processes of time and the flowing currents of the seasons: *kineitai kai rei ta panta,* that saddened the Greek, and *hinc lachrymae rerum* of Roman tears. And a New England poet, though he has an occasional page of Christian interpretation, is neo-pagan when he sets October in this line:

> The melancholy days have come, the saddest of the year.

Rather, the true poet sings gallantly with Lionel Johnson, noting courageously and clearly time's mutable panorama:

> I know
> From mortal to immortal beauty goes;
> In triumph can the whole world die.

Colors of a fleeting rainbow enliven the palette of October; but Christian eyes, far from Greek melancholy, farther still from the neo-paganism of inflated science, perceive the abiding designs that October and all seasons write into the varied scroll; against the *panta rei* of ancient sadnesses, we sing the lasting melody and harmony of the imperishable soul, *Pax Christi,* the exordium and peroration of all beauty.

COLUMNISTS

I

The jester's motley is the garb upon much that is called literature today, but we fail to find beneath it the heart of exquisite wit and the mind of dialectical skill that were the literary equipment of the Fool in medieval drama, and especially of the Shakespearian Fools. In America, said an old teacher, we are all shoddy, from our clothes to our thoughts. In our craze for production, of quantity rather than quality, our monuments soon wilt as pasteboards; and in our boastfulness over some new "department"—for instance, the "column" in our leading journals of the past fifteen years—we should be reminded that this *genre* of literary craftsmanship existed of old, often superior in manner and matter to the rushed lucubrations of many syndicated journeymen. There is nothing (or very little) new under the "Sun-Dial," or from "Bowling Green" to the "Conning Tower"; yet a few of the motley pens have proved worthy of the court dress; may their tribe increase.

Consider the Fool, let us say in the drama of King Lear, before we note some of the deserving columnists, "in the whispering galleries of the world," as Hawthorne described the newspaper.

"Where's my fool, ho?" cries the breaking heart of the King; "I think the world's asleep."

Enters the columnist of the court. With deft humor and with appropriate satire, he tries to distract the royal pain; and yet, with his double-tipped lash, he chastises the high-offending courtesans. Now with sallies of wit, now with the sharded thongs of satire, and betimes with flashes of lyric wisdom and philosophical prose, he bravely continues the service of his curative laughter:

> He that has and a little tiny wit,—
> With hey, ho, the wind and the rain,—
> Must make content with his fortunes fit
> Though the rain it raineth every day.

"This is not altogether fool, my lord," says Kent for the rest of us, learning a philosophy.

Now this is, or ought to be, the purpose and the performance of the present-day columnist in the courts of journalism. He is not, therefore, a new man either in the essence of his vocation or in the technique of his craft, although the commercial efficiency of the press-syndicates affords the modern writer a large audience, watchful and waiting. In the externals of the mode, far away among originals, we find Greek fragments of such things: the *epigrammata* of Stesichorus, of Simonides and of Bacchylides seem like classic patches serviceable for our best columns. Fragments, too, from the later Latins, like the epigrams of Terence and Martial, continue the tradition. Indeed our latest proverbs, whether in verse or prose in the modern column, are often but hurried echoes from old patient voices. Said Bacchylides (500 B.C.)—and the great Clement of Alexandria (200 A.D.) referred to his saying—"Poet is heir to poet, now as of yore; for in sooth 'tis no light task to find the gates of virgin song."

Again, in the English tradition, what a cloud of classic writers may be summoned! If Pope and Dryden did not appear daily with a column of their couplets, a month was none too tedious to wait for the full stick of their verse. And what were the Addison papers in the *Spectator* but glorious columns, now garnered in books that the academic world waits upon. "I have a dark suspicion," writes Mr. Chesterton, "that a modern poet might manufacture an admirable lyric out of almost every line of Pope."

And in the American school, fifty years before our present specialized columnist, what excellence

we had of the craft in the work of Oliver Wendell
Holmes and Eugene Field. Without the assured
space of a daily column, they were the autocrats
of the breakfast table and the commentators under
the evening lamp, *noctes coenaeque deum*, ambrosial nights, indeed. The eastern Doctor merrily
dropped the sugar of wit and philosophy into the
tea-cups, now in scholarly tones and again in
Yankee dialect; and the western balladist sang in
many dialects his columns of humor about the man
of the street or the miner in the camp—the Man
that Worked with Dana on the New York *Sun*,
and the honest chef of Casey's Table d'Hôte. And
in line with these bookmen columnists, many a
humble weekly, and an occasional daily, paved the
way for the present method. Who recalls the
facility and fertility of the Benztown Bard with
his yard of verse that appeared daily in the Baltimore *Sun* over twenty years ago? And who has
yet forgotten the unique space that T. A. Daly
filled every week in the Philadelphia *Standard and
Times?* Occasionally the town weekly was able
to play Maecenas to its village bard, though for the
most part he was the "scissors-and-glue-pot editor"
to supply the demand. If his reading public was
the *hoi polloi,* he was expert enough, however, to
select the *analecta* that would merit the delight of

refined society. "A Snapper-up of Unconsidered Trifles," he was entitled in the *Pilot* during the splendid years of Boyle O'Reilly and Jeffrey Roche; and what a wealth of sense and nonsense, jest and reason, filled that merry column! O'Reilly possessed the delicacy of the Cherry-Stone artist, yet, in larger compositions, he steadily gives the "one touch of nature that makes the whole world kin," singing for the city millions, who will ever look over the skyscrapers to the energies of the cloistral country:

>I am tired of the planning and toiling
>In the crowded hives of men,
>Heart-weary of building and spoiling
>And spoiling and building again;
>And I long for the dear old river,
>Where I dreamed my youth away,
>For a dreamer lives forever,
>But a toiler dies in a day.

And if Jeffrey Roche turned out exquisite satire, as in the verse on the vase, his piquant quips in prose were worth waiting a week to enjoy. "I have heard," said he, in one of these, "that Queen Victoria has written a book of poems, but that she has given orders not to publish them until after her death. Here is one instance where I sing with all my heart, 'Long live the Queen.'"

To be ready to fill a vacant space was part of the

day's work, whether the call came to the editor with his pen or to the printer's devil with a scissors. But the departmental system which has its roots in many American departments demands the columnist to be a specialist, an expert in his own name, or apt as an overseer in selecting from other sources. Supply and demand count as in other industries. To the clicking tune of insistent presses, how can they be expected to fill the bag every day with golden nuggets of humor and wisdom? Yet if they fall short of the exquisiteness of Pindaric odes and Horatian satire, or of paragraphs from courtly jesters such as Addison and Oliver Wendell Holmes, still these American columns strive to weave into the texture of their speech and song an occasional thread of homespun philosophy and human sympathy. Now and then, even the light of supermundane things filters into the yearning of their best moods: "stretching out their hands in yearning for a farther shore," as Virgil reported of his ardent rovers. Be it noted that the best columnists of our day—a day that has somewhat slighted the Latin and Greek classics—have sedulously served their apprenticeship over models that were created in Rome and Athens; they inherit the old longings that were felt upon the Appian Way and around the Acropolis over two thousand years ago; and they are adepts in classic meters and allusions when their lighter moods comment on "the purple pageant of the passing show." The true American columnist, moreover, maintains the culture of *bonhommie*, a spirit of give and take, "having the sunny malice of a faun," bitter only against sham and pretense.

II

Consider four of them now, though the American list numbers fourscore who have worn the motley well for the courtiers and the groundlings in the columnist play. Hamlet says, as if in their regard: "Good my lord, will you see the players well bestowed? Do you hear, let them be well used; for they are the abstracts and brief chronicles of the time; after death you were better have a bad epitaph than their ill report while you live."

Two of the troupe, Bert Leston Taylor and Keith Preston, are experts in the gestures and tunes of the columnist motley. Though they have not "teamed" together—to adapt a word from vaudeville groups—they exhibit a literary kinship, having come into the craft of letters from a training in classical studies, therefore from the tradition of the humanities; and with kindred eyes of kindliness they appraise the sane things of nonsense and dispraise the serious insanity of the fads.

Take, for instance, the hysterical seriousness of the fad of free verse—the little-read school, we may safely predict that it will be called in another generation. What outcries against the poetry of the past the protagonists of this cult have made; what clamor for their present theories and unconvincing achievements! How they fit into the observing sentence that Addison wrote: "As there are none more ambitious of fame than those who are conversant in poetry, it is very natural for such as have not succeeded in it to depreciate the works of those who have." And with a lighter touch of the critic's wand, Bert Leston Taylor strokes the pompous courtiers of that group:

> Come, my Muse, let us exalt the obvious!
> Unfettered let us name
> The sum of two and two, the which
> Is four.
> This form of verse, *vers libre*, lends itself
> Exactly to our purpose,
> For obvious reasons—
> Reasons as obvious as Marie
> Corelli.
>
> Here we are as free as air, and hence
> Our airy nothings, which are
> Nothing if not airy;
> And hence we give ourselves airs.

> And air our grievances against the persons
> Who cannot see us,
> Who could not see us with a telescope
> > At Lick.

And Keith Preston, foreseeing the sure passing of the cult in a short while, sings for its epitaph:

> Of all our literary scenes,
> Saddest the sight to me,—
> The graves of little magazines
> That died to make verse free.

The verse of these columnists, even in their light satirical moods, will outlast the ill-regulated babblings of the serious modernists in verse. For the songs of the Fools in Shakespeare have been set to music by masters; and our true jesters represent learning as well as ready wit; they have memory and thought as well as words, and from the thesaurus of the world's moral utterances they serve out ethics in their doses of artistic pleasantries. Columnists, worthy of the vocation, endeavor to "see life steadily and see it whole"; and that is the function of poet and critic. Schooled in the classical traditions, craftsmen such as Taylor and Preston strove to serve the high laws of literature, as they flashed their motley at pretenders in the court of life. It is eminently fitting to repeat here what Franklin P. Adams—himself a skilled columnist in his "Conning Tower"—wrote in a preface after Taylor's death:

> Nowhere in literature have results been achieved with greater or surer simplicity. The Taylor verse is sure; in each line is the utmost effort. He used to say that if he could write a 99 per cent line in three minutes and a 100 per cent line in nine hours, or nine days, there should be no problem of conduct; that though maybe nobody would know the difference, you were writing for yourself, and nothing short of your uttermost was thinkable.

Here, surely, is a model for aspirants to this popular department of our modern journalism. Twenty years of conscientious work in versification counted well for Taylor in his art and ethics. He is typically representative of the best in this field of writing: American, strenuous and painstaking, kindly in his satire against the shams of the day and, like all true-hearted American poets, a lover of children. His *Babette Ballads* shall enter anthologies that contain Eugene Field and Whitcomb Riley and T. A. Daly. In the din of a press-room he caught musical lines, as:

> Loveliest of hills, Lucretilis:

and he always insisted on the medicinal value of

wholesome merriment, true to his own "Ballade of Old-Time Clowns."

> Where (as ballades so oft begin)
> The classic clowns of yesterday?
> Where Guillaume of the famous grin,
> And eke the gifted Gaultier?
>
> Gone, like the monarch's harlequin,
> They who tickled the common clay;
> Gone the bumpkin who owned their sway;
> Clown and rustic together sleep,
> This is the tribute we may pay:
> *It was to laugh and not to weep.*

Under the parti-colored costume of the jester, the heart of the olden Fool was often in pain as he sang out his witticisms; he was to create laughter for others, not for himself. And Keith Preston gives as a law for the humorist:

> He must not laugh at his own wheeze:
> A snuff box has no right to sneeze.

But he should sneeze, as Preston does in rhythms of sane satire, when he considers the highly advertised yet make-believe authors of the day. It used to be said that Macaulay's history was *his story;* and Preston flings his coxcomb thus at the Wells *Outline of History:*

> Bare facts and experts void of art
> Boosted bad boys like Bonaparte;
> So we acclaim in accents hearty,
> This book less expert than *ex parte.*

And of the furore, also exquisitely commercialized, in regard of one of the matinée idols in fiction—the school of effervescence and evanescence—Preston's singing critique says:

> We've found this Scott Fitzgerald chap
> A chipper charming child:
> But now he should make haste to trap
> The ducats in his dipper;
> The birds that put him on the map
> Will shortly all begin to rap,
> And flop to something flipper.

Turning from the classic "shreds and patches" and the mocking-bird levities of Taylor and Preston, we welcome another two of the troupe—Don Marquis and Christopher Morley, actors now in the higher buskin. Since we are all aware that these two worthies are better known in this year of grace for their ampler programs, surely they will not hesitate to appear in the role of columnist for this brief *entr'acte*. Have they not written entire dramas? Ask the *Old Soak*. Have they not produced novels and volumes of verse, and books of essays? Sample *The Plum Pudding*. The garrulous Polonius would be needed to catalogue the effects of their versatility: "The best actors in the world, either for tragedy, comedy, history, pastoral, pastoral-comical, historical-pastoral, tragical-historical, tragical-comical-historical-pastoral, scene individable, or poem unlimited: Seneca cannot be too heavy, nor Plautus too light. For the law of writ and the liberty, these are the only men."

Certainly Don Marquis has played well the parts of Seneca and of Plautus. He has kept the court in all the varied chuckles of laughter, now with the coxcomb of wit, now with the sure sword-thrust of profound humor. In the column made famous by him, "The Sun Dial," he allured thousands of readers to look for his "entrances and exits" before they scanned the pompous headlines of the evening news. Even Englishmen lifted the monocle of their delight toward him for the humor that "is utterly and unmistakably American in flavor," as Hugh Walpole reported for them.

But his Seneca doses are more effective in their healthful satire and in salutary blood-letting and ghost-laying. His jesting ironies wear a Gaelic external—"Erin, the tear and the smile in thine eyes"; and if there are bitter tears over the sham, the effete lassitude, the paganism of many "acts" in the drama of modern society, as in degenerate days of ancient Rome—hence the weeping tears—this American minstrel enacts cheerily the wistful optimism of a stoic, as the couplet by Bacchylides prescribes: "One canon is there, one sure way, of happiness for mortals—if one can keep a cheerful spirit throughout life."

Don Marquis is the choir-leader of his "Jesters."

We cannot help it, we are accursed
With an incorrigible mirth;—
Although we too have been saddened with the clouds that shadow
The disconsolate Earth;—
Although we too have mourned with all mankind the disillusions of the barren years;—
Although with all mankind we drink the acrid tears;—
Still, in our ultimate
Numb moments of despair,
Still, in our desolate
Bowed anguish here beneath the whips of fate,
Still, when we reach the dark way's darkest end,
And by the blind wall droop with none to friend,
Then, of a sudden,
Some perverse humor shakes us, and we laugh!
Some tricky thought will grip us, and we laugh!—

Emphasizing the perplexities of life, Don Marquis often chimes in the chant of many an unsettled school before him. Yet he escapes the gloomy sadness of Matthew Arnold, even if he does not sing, through the melancholy of Hamlet, "There's a divinity that shapes our wills." He cannot profess the hollow laughter of Omar Khayyam's sensism, nor the black negations of materialism in *De Rerum Natura* of Lucretius: but he has yet to achieve the triumphant conclusions of Francis

Columnists

Thompson, whose *Hound of Heaven* conducts the spiritual hunt on Forty-second Street as well as at Charing Cross.

Cries the Don:

> I have looked inward and seen the world;
> I have looked out upon the world
> And shuddered
> To behold myself.
>
> Through the antres of my brain
> A loud wind rushed,
> And it was black with witches
> Shrieking in pursuit of . . . me!

Whereas, Thompson sings of the pursuit:

> I fled Him, down the nights and down the days; . . .
> I fled Him, down the labyrinthine ways
> Of my own mind; and in the midst of tears
> I fled from Him, and under running laughter. . . .
>
> Nature, poor stepdame, cannot slake my drouth;
> Never did any milk of hers once bless
> My thirsting mouth. . . .
>
> Now of that long pursuit
> Comes on at hand the bruit;
> That Voice is round me like a bursting sea. . . .
>
> Halts by me that footfall;
> Is my gloom after all,
> Shade of His hand, outstretched caressingly?

Man of the street and child of the age, Don

Marquis is moreover a voice of our times. His pen at times is dipped in corrosive acids such as Juvenal used, and the first Brann of *The Iconoclast;* but his *Savage Portraits* do social service, being satiric mirrors of scorn for a gallery of parlor rogues and social scamps. At his best, however, whether in the light motley or the philosopher's cloak, mingling the useful and the sweet—*qui miscuit utile dulci,* according to the prescription of Horace, the old Latin columnist—Don Marquis is truly representative of present-day American letters. Anthologies shall tell of him in the future. Through the rainbow of tears and laughter his continued singing shall endeavor to visualize a Jacob's Ladder which rises above agnosticism and mere transient feelings to certitudes in assured consequences.

If Don Marquis has the manner of Juvenal, Christopher Morley keeps rather the tune and time of Horace. "What prevents a man," said that Latin columnist of long ago, "from telling a truth in the guise of a joke?" And under the ripple of running laughter, Morley turns the little mills of truth. He places modestly at the forefront of his collection of *Songs for a Little House* this couplet from Father Southwell:

> He that high growth on cedars did bestow,
> Gave also lowly mushrooms leave to grow.

and to his larger house in a world of friends he applies a measure from Hilaire Belloc:

> There's nothing worth the wear of winning,
> But laughter and the love of friends.

Out of a philosophy of modesty and amiableness Morley has brightened the columnist court; and he has the high atmosphere of scholarship and generous satire. What inventiveness in his modes, as when he pretends to translate a Mandarin from China, as if the Man in the Moon came down to observe quizzically the oddities in our age of faddisms; and what an echo of laughter there is in the fact that his Mandarin is translated in free verse —*exempli gratia:*

> What is the difference
> Between a Fried Egg
> And a Freud Ego?
> The same (my dear) as between
> An omelet
> And Hamlet.

And to our boasted "progress" in this vaunting age, he hears "The Old Mandarin on His Travels":

> When I visited America
> I saw two things that struck me as extraordinary:
> People packed in the subway
> Rocking uneasily on their hams,
> Endlessly studying the newspapers;

> And people packed in the movies
> Endlessly staring at the films.
> I said to myself
> If the American people ever develop Minds
> There are two great industries
> That will crash.

These columnists, therefore, are the brief chroniclers of the times, as Hamlet called the Playboys of his day. They are players in an old tradition, serving as the Greek chorus with reflections for the multitude who are watching the passing incidents in the drama of life; singing like the old street-balladists of Ireland their "staves" of enheartening songs during the storms of grief; bringing their wit and wisdom to cultural perspectives in our national life, appraising the present sense and nonsense while they praise the past in echoes of sane estimate. The columnist, worthy of the vocation, must be, as these whom we have named, active heirs of the classic treasures of the past. Hamlet, "the glass of fashion and the mould of form," was not only master of thoughtful soliloquies but of little snatches of moralizing verses out of the world's storehouse of song:

> Why, let the stricken deer go weep,
>   The hart ungalled play;
> For some must watch, while some must sleep:
>   So runs the world away.

Columnists

For underneath the motley and the jesting, the columnist who is scholar and courtier, as Hamlet was to the reading eyes of Ophelia and Horatio, will constantly call the rush-away world to the cult of Truth and Beauty: to an "adjustment" which the Mandarin of Christopher Morley desiderates:

> In your Great City
> I see, in jewellers' windows,
> Clocks that tell the guaranteed correct time;
> And in front of those clocks people halted
> Adjusting their watches.
> But suppose there were displayed, beside the street,
> Some great poem,
> Telling perfect Truth and Beauty,
> How many passengers
> Would pause to adjust their minds?

POETS' POETS

The child in early centuries of song has frequently been father to the man of later poetry. Francis Thompson loyally called Edmund Spenser the treasure-house from which many poetic disciples gathered the riches of their craft and song; yet E. Webbe (*circa* 1585) notes the dependence of Spenser on predecessors in older languages, "the works of Theocritus in Greek, or Virgil in Latin, whom he narrowly imitateth." And if Virgil, like a child in class, could raise his hand, it would be to confess that he himself had "narrowly imitated" Homer and the poetry of earlier centuries. The tradition of dependence upon the old Greek poets—let us name but two, Homer and Sophocles—carries the testimony of great poets in other literatures.

If the texts and translations of these Greek masters were deleted from the world, we could still visualize the soul of these authors, even if we could not reconstruct their bodies. Lines here and there, like bits of bones from a cave, might be gathered from commentators; the fragments might lead to an integral restoration; just as the craftsman in a side room of the British Museum may fashion with perfect accuracy the replica of a Greek temple, having for his start only a broken plinth and a line of the pediment which the excavating archeologists furnished. A scholarly collector, if he had the memory of Macaulay and the linguistic ability of Mezzofanti, could well present a similar achievement in Homer's regard. For what parcels, numerous and ample, out of Homer, direct citations and felicitous paraphrases, find lodgment in the pages of other literatures.

But it is the spirit, or the vital spark of the spirit of Homer and Sophocles, that can be most easily discovered in the revivifying appraisements of later poets. And before we advance a worthy illustration or two, and so stand our armor up for proof, let us insist that it is the soul of a great poet, a great soul, and not a mere sentimental spook, which merits perennial resurrection—everlasting, as far as time can carry it. Welcome revisitant is he, both in his own magisterial robes or come he garbed in the eulogies of other poets, thinking with them at their firesides, whispering from their balconies, with his spiritual ideals, with his motives for character which transcend in importance anything his bodily lineaments, to wit, his textual integrity, might present. It should be so; and herein the metaphysical critic, with humanistic appreciations, surpasses the physical anatomist, who is a mere philologist. For the spirituality of ethics takes precedence over the materialistic externals of aesthetics. Ethics is the elder sister in the household of art. Aesthetics, meaning sensation as the basis of the beautiful, must remain a modest serving-maid. "Obedience to law" was written over the gateway to Eden; and though invisible to the bodily eye, it should read across every temple of art, and run like a golden thread through the songs of a great poet, if he propose to have his soul endure, and, in a later day and society, serve other souls. Sydney, a name indeed in the history of criticism, says well, when estimating the author of Gorboduc: "He is full of a notable morality, which it doth most delightfully teach, and so obtain the very end of poesy." And, as another marginal note, let us remark that Francis Thompson elaborated a magnificent eulogy on Shelley's art; but Thompson limps and halts and breaks down over his analysis of Shelley's ethical content, or rather over his aesthetic void.

Returning then to the line of our text, read the partial roll-call of names that bow with reverent appreciations to Homer and Sophocles. Virgil and Horace, Dante and Keats support the canopy over Homer's triumphant march: Seneca, Corneille (let us whisper Voltaire) and Matthew Arnold are the goodly escort for Sophocles.

Remind me not that Dante and Keats are ill chosen, since they were not scholars to the Greek letter. But who shall deny that they knew the spirit, venerated the great soul of the "sovereign poet," as Dante named him; and Dante, though he venerated Virgil as "my master," calls Homer "that lord of highest song who soars like an eagle above the others." Keats, too, gave promise of a wonderful cult of the Greek bard, a promise rich in achievement had time been allowed him. From a first cursory view of those peaks and plains of song, seen merely through the glasses of Chapman, he produced that sonnet which rings like a command, "eyes right," toward Homer in every grand review of the master poets. Keats, through the perennial tribute of this sonnet, shall be cicerone for Homer in American schools, which refuse to recognize the Greek if he enter alone. Attention!

ON FIRST LOOKING INTO CHAPMAN'S HOMER

Much have I traveled in the realms of gold,
And many goodly states and kingdoms seen;
Round many western islands have I been
Which bards in fealty to Apollo hold.
Oft of one wide expanse had I been told
That deep-browed Homer ruled as his demesne;
Yet did I never breathe its pure serene

> Till I heard Chapman speak out loud and bold:
> Then felt I like some watcher of the skies
> When a new planet swims into his ken;
> Or like stout Cortez when with eagle eyes
> He stared at the Pacific—and all his men
> Looked at each other with a wild surmise—
> Silent, upon a peak in Darien.

"Applaud ye!" say we first in salute of Homer: "Encore!" for Keats. And Matthew Arnold ventures to add that Homer, though blind, had greater spaces in his vision than Balboa (whom Keats misnamed Cortez) obtained from the summit of Darien. Homer is for Arnold primarily a guide and support of character, however largely the English critic praised him on other lines, and imitated him in countless pages. The soul of the Greek master was a shield for the disciple in adversity. Witness the verification of this in the question and response of the first quatrain in Arnold's sonnet:

> Who prop, thou ask'st, in these bad days, my mind?—
> He much, the old man, who, clearest-soul'd of men,
> Saw the Wide Prospect, and the Asian Fen,
> And Tmolus hill, and Smyrna bay, though blind.

Then with a tribute to Epictetus, whom even St. Augustine hailed "the noblest Stoic," Arnold mounts higher and places the chief laurel on the brow of Sophocles. The lyric art of this Greek,

as legend asserts of an ode in his Colonus, amazed
a supreme court in law; his dramatic genius thrilled
and thrilled again a people of exquisite discernment; his ethical content is the soul that endures,
and wears, *salva reverentia,* like the Lorica of St.
Patrick, for characters who live at least the natural
law. It is the spirit of that majestic Greek, more
stately than the Ghost to Hamlet, that walks the
platform upon which Arnold presents Sophocles:

> Whose even-balanced soul,
> From first youth tested up to extreme old age,
> Business could not make dull, nor passion wild;
> Who saw life steadily, and saw it whole;
> The mellow glory of the Attic stage,
> Singer of sweet Colonus, and its child.

We need not go searching for embellishments for
this mise en scene; embroidery is superfluous. Imi-
tators of the Greek, who labored to present the
later stage with adaptations of Sophoclean characters—Seneca, Corneille, Dryden and Voltaire—let
them pass with their courtesy. Prophecy in regard
of his art, Ovid makes without hazard:

> Nulla Sophocleo veniet jactura cothurno.

Arnold is at one end of the arch of true praise;
and at the other is Phrynicus, contemporary of

Sophocles, singing of him, as Campbell reports the fragment:

> The happy child of sad Melpomene
> To whom long life brought no calamity,
> To crown his works Genius and Fortune blend,
> And Death has sealed them with a peaceful end.

Return we then to the "sovereign poet," to that remote predecessor of Sophocles, to Homer, the seer of "the wide prospect." His soul, gleaming in a hundred places, proves its immortal stuff by the testimony of great critics in all ages. Horace among the Latins almost two thousand years ago: Horace, man of the street, yet courtier and courted, pupil of many modes of Greek verse, Horace the philosopher goes to Homer for a lecture on the ethical quality of great poetry. First, note this Latin academician's prescription for worthy poetry: "This was what was meant by Wisdom in old days: to separate the rights of one from the rights of all, divine things from common, to forbid lawless love and prescribe rules of wedded life, to build cities and grave laws on wooden tables." And with thoughts of Homer before him, with his name ready for use as an illustration, Horace continues: "It was so that poets sung, and their song won the honor and the name of divine. In song oracles were given, and men were guided in the ways of life; the favor of kings was courted in strains learnt of the Muses, and amusement was found to crown the close of long toil." Passing from this Epistle to the Pisos to another letter, the second in the first book of Horace's Epistles, hearken to the more direct lecture with Homer for the text. It commands attention not merely for its revelation of the heart and soul of the *Iliad* and *Odyssey,* but for its critical skill as well. It urges to the lips a wish that we had such books to review today, and such critics to review them. Homer, so the Latin disciple insists, is primarily, a book of morals: "While you have been practicing in declamation at Rome, Lollius Maximus, I have been reading again at Praeneste the story-teller of the Trojan War; who shows us what is fair, what is foul, what is profitable, what not, more plainly and better than a Chrysippus or a Crantor."

The Stoic lecturers of that day, therefore, whether in the temples or on the Via Sacra, could not compare with the truer and more fascinating expression of doctrine found in Homer, his ethics vitalizing his esthetics. And the synopsis which Horace gives runs memorable with lines of the value of accepted proverbs, twenty of them as striking and as comprehensive as these:

> Quidquid delirant reges plectuntur Achivi.
> Seditione, dolis, scelere atque libidine et ira
> Iliacos intra muros peccatur et extra.

Let us recommend that an English version of these lines run as a mural memento around the chamber of the League of Nations: "For the delirium of Prime Ministers, the people are made to suffer. Faction, craft, wickedness, and the lust and anger from which it springs—these are the sources of wrongdoing within the walls of Troy and beyond them."

Thereupon comes the keen synopsis of the *Odyssey;* again the insistent commendation of the moral value, of the undying soul-attributes of that book. "Again, of the power of virtue and of wisdom, Homer has given us a profitable example in Ulysses." What are we—Horace intones the solemn question from the heart of the *Odyssey*—but mere ciphers in comparison with that hero? Purchase at any cost, and at once, this Homeric character. He who has begun the task has half done it. Have the courage to be wise.

Such gleams of Homer's soul, in the investiture of the *Odyssey*, may have been the happy fortune of Tennyson, the inspiration of his fragment on Ulysses—albeit some critics of the Victorian poet refer to lines in the twenty-sixth canto of Dante's *Inferno* for the germinal root. But almost the entire Victorian school, as did the Augustan school with Virgil for chief marshal, flocked to the *Iliad* and *Odyssey* for observations and studies, for art that is no mere iridescent shell, but an embodiment of a spirit that still virtuously haunts our best aspirations. Compel the poetasters of our literature of mimicry—those clamorous monodists "of sex and soul," whom Joyce Kilmer ably satirized—to obey this command of Alexander Pope:

> Be Homer's works your study and delight,
> Read them by day, and meditate by night;
> Thence form your judgment, thence your maxims bring,
> And trace the Muses upward to their spring.
> Still with the text itself compared, his text peruse;
> And let your comment be the Mantuan Muse.

LITERARY VAUDEVILLIANS

Every age produces its burlesque critics of men and manners. For imitation is instinctive in man from infancy, said Aristotle in an earlier era, albeit the fact is earlier than the sentence in which he stated it. The pity is that the infantile proclivity runs higher into extravagance as the contemporaneous degree in the nobler arts drops lower in the scale of worth. Too often in the history of art the pendulum has swung from symphony to cacophony, from delightful joys to frightful jazz. The mimicries beget catbirds that chase away the true mocking-bird, the polyglot mime. The *patres graviores* find it difficult to raise a voice against the *enfants terribles*. Yet in "the good old days," the artistic communities, like the New England villages appointing a sealer of weights and measures for the farmers, directed the crops of Comedy. Even in Aristotle's day, said he, "it was not till late that comedy was authorized by the magistrate, and carried on at the public expense; it was at first a private and voluntary exhibition." This magisterial function sometimes creeps forth from our editorial conservatists. For the editor is, and ought to be by profession, a critic; and a critic, as Sainte-Beuve explained, is only "the secretary of the public—though a secretary who does not wait to be dictated to, but each morning divines and redacts the general opinion."

Let us carry these observations for proof to a present-day scene. A recent incident in France afforded a peg on which a few of our judicious editors hung up a column of comment against one of the manifestations of cheap flippancy in our modern world. An American dancer in a Paris music hall was doing his clownish antics to a mutilated melody of the "Marseillaise"; the indignant French audience howled him from the stage; he went into eclipse behind the curtain, and the manager quickly appeared and apologized. "The 'Marseillaise' shall not be parodied," said the Prefect: *Vive la France!*

In sympathy with this action, editorial comment proceeded to expatiate upon the overdose of parodying which is so characteristic of our day. "Tawdry imitations and grotesque distortions of music and literature, endeared to us by origin, age or association, pass too often for cleverness," is their general regret; and "the finer a poem or a passage of prose is, the more liable it is to cheap burlesquing."

These animadversions, worthy as they are, are nothing new; they have been repeated and stressed in other times and countries which were suffering from a lack of sincerity in life and of inspiration in the arts. *Natio comoeda est*—we are a nation of comedians—Juvenal cried out in a day when pagan Rome in life and letters was what a great part of America is today. To escape from the meretricious splashes in art and from cheap glibnesses in life and letters, Juvenal sought a remote countryside; there he might enjoy the simple truths of nature and fling his vitriolic censure back at a degenerating society—an indignant Don of nineteen hundred years ago, writing as the Don Marquis of today his "Savage Portraits" against a nation of comedians in social life, and of flippant parodists in art.

And in a later age, from an academic place, so to speak, Ruskin put his finger upon the pulse of his time: "I suppose the chief bar to the action of imagination and stop to all greatness in this present age of ours is its mean and shallow love of jest." If this were true of England then, it is truer of America now. Glib cleverness is accorded mistaken appraisals amongst us; we advertise it as an asset, and it is leaving us bankrupt in a debris of artistic fragments. The potpourri is dished out on every

Literary Vaudevillians 51

side. "Yes, we have no . . ." is a typical bit of potsherd made popular for the spirit of the times by stealing that many notes of "Halleluia"—a spirit which knows that much of Handel's music, and goes too far by going that far. Shreds and patches, like the false king upon Hamlet's throne, it is the spirit of a plaster age, howsoever euphoniously a surface analysis may call it the "Plastic Age." It is a skeleton in the closet of American education, or rather of present methods in our accented system of education—those skim-milk processes which are devoid of effort and labor and patience, which, therefore, cannot be the feeding ground of inspiration, not only of art, but of the art of true humor.

None of us wishes to deplore the genuine spirit of wit and laughter which makes for sanity and sanctity in national life and even in art appreciations. What prevents a man from telling a truth in the guise of a joke?—was a Horatian question for the salon and boulevard two thousand years ago. And the world keeps answering in the truth of a sensible couplet:

> A little nonsense now and then
> Is relished by the best of men.

There is art in the artlessness of Will Rogers, as

there was, to a better degree, in the humorists of a preceding generation—Josh Billings and "Mr. Dooley," who gave to their funniness certain rich echoes out of literature and philosophy. Likewise the grotesque buffoonery of some daily cartoons may have salutary processes in their wholesome satire: for the lash of scorn is deserved upon the folly of those who try to keep up with the Joneses, for such as have not the saving common sense to sing with the city-sick in Whitcomb Riley's ballad,

> Let's go a-visitin' back to Griggsby's Station,
> Back where we used to be so happy and so poor.

Moreover, the lance of derision can let out bad blood for that pitiful class of new-rich, who are so pretentious in bringing up father, the quondam brick-layer, who now inhabits a "brownstone mansion" on Fifth Avenue and piteously croons the *Come-all-ye* many a day,—

> An' I long for me mornin's mornin',
> In Shanahan's ould shebeen.

These parodies in life and art are not without their service in the national comedy. Communal laughter can be a medicine for the common good. Philosophy and even theology have chapters of reason on the virtue of well-seasoned wit: *Eutrapelia,* they call it, as the ancient Greeks did. There is something rotten in the Denmarks of society when an exhilarating witticism can raise only a cynical curl of the lip or a stoical smile; the heart must be out of joint with the times of healthy life. Trouble must be gnawing at the soul, and spiritual ennui around it like a cloud. Like many another heart of courage, Louise Imogen Guiney could sing with a merry voice, though "sick with the impact of eternity"; while "Yon Cassius has a lean and hungry look" was Caesar's description of one whom he considered to be a disgruntled grouch:

> Seldom he smiles, and smiles in such a sort
> As if he mock'd himself and scorn'd his spirit
> That could be moved to smile at any thing.

Life is capable of true laughter only when it is lived upon the ground of holiness and of those principles which make possible and frequent the laughter of the saints, *risus ille sanctorum*, which is a cure for effete society. And great art, too, can decorously indulge in winking *humoresques*, like the gargoyles squinting from beneath cathedral roofs.

But the facile abundance of our present-day wit, cheap and vulgar, is another thing. Our current parade of vaudeville smartness lacks the very name of humor; it is the debased coinage of puerility, not the legitimate currency of real humanity. It would be but another joke to try to stop these counterfeits by law, to introduce an Eighteenth-and-a-half Amendment to suppress them. Yet public opinion ought to stand up like the French Prefect for his "Marseillaise" and drive these boot-black professors of jazz in music, of parodies in literature, of irreverence in conduct, to some eclipsed Charleston on the other side of the sterile moon. Perhaps our editors, like the right-thinking chorus in a Greek drama, will continue their approved animadversions.

These secretaries of the public, however, who paused to comment upon the French incident, seemed hesitant about mentioning specific cases deserving of American censure. A few of them signaled Mr. Mencken as one of the cheap offenders in these parrot parodies, possibly because he is alien to the Nordic set. Mr. Mencken needs no added hand to hold a brief for him; he is fully capable of presenting his own briefs in full length; moreover, much of his satire is serviceable against the cant and superficiality of the pretending castle-party. They cite a sentence of his burlesque on Lincoln's Gettysburg address; yet they could more readily find some "one-hundred percent" Americans who have traves-

Literary Vaudevillians 55

tied the Psalms of David, and the Beatitudes of the Mount. Whatever be the extent of Mr. Mencken's censurable parodying, he cannot in this particular regard, aside from all other issues, "hold a candle" to the larger offenses of Mark Twain, whose mimicries—no small quota of his writings—are mere Barnum-and-Bailey buffooneries. The tin-pan amusement, for instance, of his *Connecticut Yankee at the Court of King Arthur* lives on chiefly because it has commercial possibilities. How different the cause that perpetuates a great satire on old romance and chivalry—the classic humorist, Cervantes, in his *Don Quixote*, which is an epic of humor, and yet a national cultural force, giving over two hundred and fifty proverbs to the hearts and lips of the people.

One other example: the parodists who offend these editors do not sprawl about a three-ring circus of literary buffoonery any more nimbly and persistently than some of those in the established academy, than, let us say, Professor Stephen Leacock, who (thanking him for an occasional laugh, some "palpable hits") has travestied not a few of the noblest things in English literature. If such antics are found in the professorial dry-wood, what must we expect from the student greeneries? Were these conservative editors shocked twenty years ago when a student publication of a Middle West university celebrated the huge endowments of its benefactor to the tune of a meeting-house hymn:

> Praise John from whom all blessings flow,
> Praise him oil creatures here below.

This irreverent cackle of college goslings is part of a heritage from the antecedent irreverence of the geese. An American professor of an American college, in an American magazine, unblushingly states, "The college or university should not concern itself with striving to perpetuate a convention like pre-marital chastity." Can wonder blush, therefore, at the degenerate ravings of much that passes for "college humor," the ribald jests of poetic lice and license from the *garcons* of a smutty *cuisine*, who would be kicked out of Dinty Moore's back-parlor, and, if they showed up in the pages of the old dime novels, would fall before the bullets of Deadwood Dick. "Our youngsters shall be as we are," said Juvenal to the profligate humor of ancient Rome. A Juvenal is needed as American professor in a modern American magazine. Was it Goethe (or Schiller?) who said that the Reformation put back the progress of the human mind for centuries, "by giving every man the right to express an opinion without giving him the power to form one."

Literary Vaudevillians 57

When a nation loses its sense of reverence for sacred realities and relationships, it is already far advanced in processes of national decay. Art and literature, and true humor in their neighborhood, are defenses of a nation's life in every department—religious, social, political and financial. They are tones of that constant battle cry that should be in every patriotic heart, as of old—*pro aris et focis*—for our altars and our hearthfires. For these sacred objects, the art and literature of a century creates its highest memorials: and the spirit of culture, whose heart beats to the pulse of reverence, will insure them against the cachinnations of flippant jest and from the parodies that are vulgarizations of debased talent. Call back the exiled Juvenals and change their cynicism into friendly laughter:

> From quiet homes and first beginning,
> Out to the undiscovered ends,
> There's nothing worth the wear of winning,
> But laughter and the love of friends.

GAS-HOUSE POETRY

There is a bleak-looking structure down in the valley, a huge cylindrical blur across the landscape, a vaunting monster amid gentle cottages in the village. It is the gas house. The chimney, like a Bolshevist pencil stuck boldly into the air, emits occasionally a smear of flame, the explosive puff from the exhaust. The flare-up attracts no notice in the clear, steady light of daytime, but in the darkness of night the sudden brilliance startles the itinerants of the neighborhood.

There you have the imagistic symbol of the free-versist; there is the technique of ninety per cent of what is clamorously termed "modern poetry"—the detached, the occasional flare-up, like some scarlet word or crimson line rising out of a waste of words in the ode or lyric. It strikes attention for a moment, only this and nothing more; and quickly it dies away in the dissipation of multiplied nothingnesses and is buried deep in the circumambient waste of commonplace lines and the flat marshes of banalities. Free verse (I must repeat that I am looking at what is boisterously called "the modern school") resembles art only as a scarecrow stands for a man; it is a thing, not a king, of shreds and patches. It has unity only "by accident," like the oneness of a cord of wood; but it is not the tree, structurally organized, with a vital in-ness through root and trunk, flower and fruit.

Let it not be imagined here, as pedantic free-versists may shout back, that we postulate for poetry or even good verse the mechanics of rhyme and fixed rhythm, either the elaborate rhyme-system of Gaelic poetry (800 A.D.), or the rhythmical maneuvers of Greek choruses (450 B.C.). Every amateur reader in English literature knows that there are abundant specimens of good poetry, on either side of the Victorian period, without rhyme or "footed" rhythms: Coventry Patmore with "The Toys," for instance, and Joyce Kilmer with "A Blue Valentine." But these odes and lyrics and ballads do not lack the processes of organization, the norms of art, the vital energy of living emotions and ecstasy, the wholesome exultation in the lyrism and an eye in fine frenzy rolling. This is the test of the poet—that he should see life steadily and see it whole, as Arnold said of Sophocles.

Let us be honest and admit that the ecstasy of much of the free verse today seems to be a replica of the pitiable mouthings, the insistent ejaculations of inmates in an insane asylum, the lyrism of a psychiatric ward. The mechanics of "the average" free-verse product seems to have the movement of a St. Vitus dance, done in a sort of vertigo. This modern school needs the vitriolic censure of a Juvenal, who even cried over the quantities of parchment wasted by the "moderns" of his day. Or should we take the attitude of the laughing philosopher at the patchy pomposity of our modernistic versifiers, at their supercilious scoffing of the three R's—rhyme, rhythm and reason; and let us add another, restraint; for true art selects, elects and perfects on the ground of restraint.

As a laughing philosopher, Mr. Chesterton punctures the mummer manners of these moderns. From his essay on Pope, written long ago, a reader might have felt that Mr. Chesterton was exaggerating the excess baggage of the free-versist; but the twenty years between his laugh and the present exhibitions show that he was looking clearly at the horizon. If in that green wood the prospect was so ridiculous, what is it now in the dry! Said Chesterton: "Supposing that a lyric poet of the new school really had to deal with such an idea as that expressed in Pope's line about Man:

A being darkly wise and rudely great.

Gas-House Poetry

Is it really so certain that he would go deeper into the matter than that old antithetical jingle goes? . . . The contemporary poet, in his elaborately ornamental book of verses, would produce something like the following:

> A creature
> Of feature
> More dark, more dark, more dark than skies,
> Yea, darkly wise, yea, darkly wise;
> Darkly wise as a formless fate.
> And if he be great,
> If he be great, then rudely great,
> Rudely great as a plough that plies,
> And darkly wise, and darkly wise."

One might suppose, as I have said, that Mr. Chesterton was jesting with the manner; but we find his contention verified in repeated pages of free verse, almost every second page. Anthologies, with mock heroic seriousness, parade them. Here is a typical one (I do not give the author's name, for I know that he has done verse that has not "this freedom"):

> We have a one-room home,
> You have a two-room, three-room, four-room.
> We have a one-room home
> because a one-room home is all we have.
> We have a one-room home
> because a one-room home holds all we have.
> We have a one-room home

> because we do not want
> a two-room, three-room, four-room.
> If we had a two-room, three-room, four-room
> we would need more than a one-room home.
> We have a one-room home.
> We like a one-room home.

Now if that is mid-Broadway manner (and it is selected from an anthology called *Today's Poetry*), give us back the mid-Victorian at its full, or Celtic twilight in all its dimness, or puffs of mythology from old Parnassus. If it is a cradle-song, for the author places it among "Berceuse Ariettes," it is better adapted for a tipster rocking a boat.

Again, in the unabashed apologetics of the free-versist, the claim is made that their matter and manner "reflect contemporary life." Bless the mark! What has most of the poetry of our Western world done in the past but faithfully reflect the life of its day, breathing the spirit of the age, copying from the body of the times the tone and gestures to the manner born? I say most of that poetry; for, of course, the allegorical and romantic forms, in lyric or epic, aim at idealizations. Must we know contemporary life only in its freckles, men only with abnormal idiosyncrasies, roads only with mud, over which the poet must not throw his Walter Raleigh cloak? Is contemporary life merely

Gas-House Poetry

a body with skin-blotches, and no soul to it capable of rational exaltations and courageous aspirations?

More specifically, take two themes that are frequent types of the material affected by these parodists of so-called contemporary life: a broken-hearted girl, suicide in the Thames or the Seine; and again, a frail woman working in "sweat-shop" conditions. Surely this is their common matter; yet life, even before our contemporaries, has had numerous instances of these tragic and sorrowful conditions. Compare, or rather contrast, the treatment of these themes by the free-versist and the genuine poet. From the former, what hysterical shrieks, what scarlet flashes, what unavailing repetitions and vulgar affectation of sordidness, unavailing for the living or the dying or the dead. On the other page, witness the service of poetry when it has to deal with those motifs. The reader may find the very examples in two lyrical ballads by Thomas Hood, "The Bridge of Sighs" and "The Song of the Shirt." Since they are too lengthy for present insertion here, I must ask the reader to review these two specimens and see how poetry treats themes that are maltreated by free verse. Moreover, be it noted that Hood was no mid-, but pre-Victorian. There are repetitions of word or phrase; note, however, that the reiterations count

into an artistic growth and progress. Here are
withal rhyme, rhythm, reason and restraint: and
what healthy tones are here embodied for sociological culture; what pity, that covers the dead with
graceful feeling and enheartens the living for better
things. Did not "The Song of the Shirt" bring
about a Parliamentary reform of conditions among
tenement workers?

>   Oh, Men, with Sisters dear!
>   Oh, Men with Mothers and Wives!
> It is not linen you're wearing out
>   But human creatures' lives!
>   Stitch—stitch—stitch,
>   In poverty, hunger, and dirt,
> Sewing at once, with a double thread,
>   A Shroud as well as a Shirt.

One more sample in the contrast will suffice.
Who does not know Lamb's "The Old Familiar
Faces"? It is and is likely to be in every well-
selected anthology. It has no rhyme, it moves in
varying rhythm; yet it is not free verse, for it contains "the thing" that is of the essence of poetry:

> I have had playmates, I have had companions,
> In my days of childhood, in my joyful school-days;
> All, all are gone, the old familiar faces.

> Ghost-like I paced round the haunts of my childhood,
> Earth seemed a desert I was bound to traverse,
> Seeking to find the old familiar faces.

Gas-House Poetry

Let a modern try to improve on that and what is the result? We do not have to search Mr. Chesterton for the response, for we can find the "effort" done, and, I may presume, achieved with the pompous self-satisfaction of the modern school in the *Spoon River Anthology*. Lamb's poem sings its universal appeal under a few general statements; and the Spoon River verse gurgles waterishly in its unappealing details, as, for instance, this first dip into it:

> Where are Elmer, Herman, Bert, Tom and Charley,
> The weak of will, the strong of arm, the clown,
>   the boozer, the fighter?
> All, all are sleeping on the hill.
> One passed in a fever,
> One was burned in a mine,
> One was killed in a brawl,
> One died in a jail.
> One fell from a bridge toiling for children and wife—
> All, all are sleeping, sleeping, sleeping on the hill.
> Where are Ella, Kate, Mag, Lizzie and Edith,
> The tender heart, the simple soul, the loud, the proud,
>   the happy one?
> All, all are sleeping on the hill.

Since that is a page of the modern school, let us return to the ancients with their cesuras and iambics, and to the formal couplets of Pope and Dryden: Since that is freedom, let us have the slavery of old approved laws of the art of literature. Verslibrism, which is the ritual of much of the modern school, seems to be a disposition against laws in every department—artistic, grammatical, ethical and religious. It protests the restraint of the artist's brush or chisel; it employs only a kodak to go slumming. Its images and diction belong to a world which has drifted from calm thinking, from endurance in labor, from sanity in appreciation. Free verse is in the class with music that is jazz, with dress that is bizarre, with conduct that is burlesque. Like the gas-house flare, it gives a spectral glow for a moment; but the darkness of night continues. These bounders of the modern school contribute nothing permanent to the delightful thoughts or the cultural adages of mankind. To quote the affable Bert Leston Taylor:

> I read a great deal of vers libre,
> And images scan by the score,
> But never a line,
> Be it ever so fine,
> Is added to memory's store.

Yet this is a test of great poetry, namely, that it brings forth, in beauty of expression, thoughts worthy of the memory of mankind; as Newman says of a great author: "He expresses what all feel but all cannot say; and his sayings pass into proverbs among his people, and his phrases become

Gas-House Poetry

household words and idioms of their daily speech, which is tesselated with the rich fragments of his language, as we see in foreign lands the marbles of Roman grandeur worked into the walls and pavements of modern palaces."

Fifty years hence the present hubbub of the so-called modern school will not be noticed in the anthologies, except for archeological wonderment. But many of the mid-Victorians will be there; and, in goodly numbers, the despised "artificialities" of the Age of Classicism, and the sneered-at lyrics of the Caroline and Elizabethan periods. The modern school is already old. The ephemeral glare of the gas house is dead. The stars still shine.

THE GENEARCHS OF LOUISE IMOGEN GUINEY

It is something to be a Don or a Mac—the son of somebody. Good men and true, with pardonable pride peer across the valleys of time, eager to hail their kin who went before. Tennyson's line from "Ulysses," "I am a part of all that I have met," may be modestly repeated by anybody who has a mental and moral report to make of himself. If the genealogical retrospect is gratifying, it should inspire the scion of the heritage toward prospects high and firm with resolution. The keynote of that high call can thrill the heart of any humble lad, and drill him to the step of chivalry, a fellow-at-arms with Louise Imogen Guiney's "Knight Errant."

> Spirits of old that bore me,
> And set me, meek of mind,
> Between great dreams before me,
> And deeds as great behind,
> Knowing humanity my star
> As first abroad I ride,
> Shall help me wear with every scar
> Honor at eventide.

> Let claws of lightning clutch me
> From summer's groaning cloud
> Or ever malice touch me
> And glory make me proud.
> Oh, give my youth, my faith, my sword,
> Choice of the heart's desire:
> A short life in the saddle, Lord,
> Not long life by the fire.

In many of her letters explicitly, and implicitly in many of her poems, Louise Imogen Guiney is an admirable witness to that ethnological trait of character and culture, namely, devotion to one's ancestry, veneration for the memories of one's family. Far from any tinge of pedantry, but exquisitely colored with the merry graces of filial piety, Miss Guiney lovingly gathered and noted her racial *patrins*—to use a word made familiar to her academic following in her book of charming essays under that title, the foreword elucidating the word: "A *patrin*, according to *Romano Lavo-Lil*, is a Gypsy trail: handfuls of leaves or grass cast by Gypsies on the road, to denote, to those behind, the way which they have taken."

In that volume, which is the work of a merry philosopher as well as of an erudite academician, one chapter, "On the Ethics of Descent," lays a loving finger on the pulse of the problem: "The truth is, we belong, from the beginning, to many masters, and are unspeakably beholden to the forming hands of the phenomena of the universe, rather than to the ties of blood." Recognize what the spider did for Bruce, the falling apple for Newton, the heavenly voice, *Tolle, lege,* for Saint Augustine; even a typical superman, Alexander, of fact and legend, could attest that he owed no more to his father, Philip, than to his preceptor, Aristotle. This insistence on self-growth and on the elective processes of character is ardent verse as well as pointed prose in Miss Guiney's thought: a guidon, for the soul's obedience, to develop "the primordial star," that Image to which man was created. To her poet's question, "Whence shall I take my law?" she answers:

> Neither from sires or sons,
> Nor the delivered ones,
> Holy, invoked with awe.
> Rather, dredge the divine
> Out of thine own poor dust,
> Feebly to speak and shine.
> Schools shall be as they are:
> Be thou truer, and stray
> Alone, intent, and away,
> In a savage wild to obey
> Some dim primordial star.

But a bird in the hand of actual conduct is worth two in the bush of philosophizing theory; and though Miss Guiney elaborated with sunny erudition many an enheartening paragraph upon the cultural values of one's antecedents, her devotional regard toward her "line" of ancestors—"my *preux chevalier* of a father" especially—is one of the most fascinating phases of her distinguished character. The spirit of that devotion gleams like a golden thread through much of her poetry, that poetry of which Alice Brown says loyally and judiciously, "She has done the most authentic and exquisite verse America has yet produced." And it is not a far-fetched effort for a title to say that Miss Guiney's volume could be called "The Soldier Songs of a Soldier's Daughter." The military metaphors in her poetry are consistent embellishments from her own heart of knight-errantry, and in the inheritance she had from many a field of honor. "My grandfather and great gran', too, were 'out' in the '98; and the old man had been 'out' in the '45. I hope to make his acquaintance in the sojer-boy's Paradise, which is my bourne, if I be good," was one of her merry sayings of a retrospect.

These brief allusions, brief but beautiful in their loving wistfulness, whisper forth in many of her letters. From Boston to Marseilles was a genealogical path which she knew by heart. The first, perhaps, of these *notanda,* a chapter of biographical laughter, as it were, appears in a letter to Mary Elizabeth Blake, who in those nineties was a poet, winning honors not merely in the *Pilot* but also among the set of which Oliver Wendell Holmes was the poet of the breakfast table and the cicerone of many Elsie Venners. Whether Mrs. Blake was preparing to write a chapter about Miss Guiney, or what was the reason for the communicated *data,* is not discoverable now. The envelope merely stated: "Notes toward the Life and Crimes of L. I. G. By her Pal, Mary Elizabeth Blake: C. W. Moulton, Buffalo, 1892." And the letter, in the exquisite handwriting of the merry Louise, reads, in part:

> I date from 1861, and am very much my father's daughter. Ancestry, solid Irish, with a man from Marseilles at four generations remove. Nobody of note on the family shrub; it is to be presumed that the stock was honest. Education in schools, now public, now private, all the way up; violent antipathy to it developed early; what there is of it, picturesquely imperfect. Took to literature, as I never got an offer from a circus, or the War Dept. Have had great fun at it, and purpose to have more. Think hard and work

slow; although, as the fat Lady Jane says, "Altho' you wouldn't say so."

That she was very much her father's daughter is the lifelong insistence of her memory and her pen. In a memorable essay about him which she wrote in 1896 for the Holy Cross *Purple*—Patrick Robert Guiney matriculated at Holy Cross in 1854—she gives a report that makes the reader "stand at attention" during the filial recital. She knew not only his birthplace, Parkstown, Tipperary, but that "he came of curiously mixed blood, and belonged to an adventurous and early-dying family: people always breaking away from their pleasant fields, and putting forth to the sea, or 'to the warres.'" She was schooled in his school-boy stories, hallowed or humorous; "he loved Holy Cross, and he was happy there; though he was once known to remark roguishly in after-life, that in his day it was the Alma Mater of a few full minds and many empty stomachs!" Grade by grade she could read off the details of his service in the Civil War—Governor Andrew sending him out as lieutenant with the Ninth Massachusetts, which later, as colonel, "he led more than thirty times to battle, and spurred to its most heroic achievement at Gaines Mills"; and at the end, "his promotion to the Brevet Brigadier Generalship 'for gallant and meritorious conduct

on the field,' was given with the proud endorsement
of Charles Sumner, of Adjutant-General Schouler,
and of others as famous and as beloved." The
wound which he had received at the Wilderness,
"full in the forehead, the terrible wound," touched
his remaining thirteen years with constant pain, "a
strange exchange for the outlook of his masterful
youth . . . this life, 'hidden with Christ in God,'
he endured not without thanksgiving and a certain
ultimate satisfaction." To that well-beloved career,
death placed the final period on March 21, 1877:
"there at his desk, in his usual cheery poor health,
with daffodils in a glass before him, and Shakespeare's smiling salute to them upon his lips. . . .
In an hour afterwards he was dead. Crossing the
square toward his house, he had sudden warning,
by a slight spurt of blood to his lips. He took off
his hat and knelt down by a tree: his loyal and
instinctive way of meeting his Lord. A child play-
ing near, who knew him, was the first to reach his
side; but already he was no more." And finally
follow this pilgrim daughter (who could call herself "his own young Amazon" when she recalled
the Colonel's playtimes with a company of martial
small boys whom he used to drill at Green Hill),
follow her final sentence at the shrine of this great
devotion to her father: "His memory is altogether

The Genearchs of Louise Imogen Guiney 75

wholesome. Where he stands it is clear air. Whenever the Church and State have their final roll calls, and count in, though with so different understanding, their elect who 'hungered and thirsted after justice,' the good knight of Boston who was my father will be remembered."

These several citations are not given here for the purpose of making a facile reference to an out-of-the-way essay; rather are they documentary footnotes not only for exhibiting her intense admiration for the *beau idéal* that her father was, but for explaining that "passion for perfection" which is the chivalrous soul of her poetry. Hamlet, the discerning critics like to say, had found his ideal realized in his father, and consequently, at his father's sudden taking-away, the young Prince was at a loss how to go on, how to adjust himself to the forceful and calamitous circumstances which came to meet him, his rich mentality prone to indecisiveness when practical issues were demanding his will. But Louise Guiney, at sixteen years of age, losing a father who was likewise an ideal realized, allowed no pause in her processes of mental and moral growth. In her "Sanctuary"—

> Hither Felicity
> Doth climb to me,

she could revel in the constant pursuit of intellectual treasures and, what was higher, the self-discipline of character; yet she did not become an aloof recluse like one of a generation before her in American letters—Emily Dickinson of exquisite epistles both in prose and verse. Of her soldier sire she could repeat the words and live them, which Father Robert Fulton spoke in the funeral eulogy: "General Guiney's I regard as a very perfect character. He conformed himself not only to what is lawful, but to what is great and fitting. He tamed and attached to himself the severer ideal." This thought is the very breath of her "Talisman."

> Take Temperance to thy breast,
> While yet is the hour of choosing,
> As arbitress exquisite
> Of all that shall thee betide;
> For better than fortune's best
> Is mastery in the using,
> And sweeter than anything sweet
> The art to lay it aside.

The eye of her heart went back to that fatherly influence through her entire life. "Loving salutations to my father's Holy Cross," was one of the last messages from her; and finding an incident in a poor novel, *The Wedding Bells of Glendalough*, which is based upon the circumstance of her father's death, she wrote elatedly to the author, "I lit almost

The Genearchs of Louise Imogen Guiney 77

at once, by accident on the scene of your Colonel Plunket's death. Ah! I owe all my best to that Holy Cross undergrad, bless him!" But a poem is the exquisite—and how poignant!—testimony to the soul of memory that "outlived all other joys," a poem that appeared almost forty years after her Soldier's death; and since it occurs only in another out-of-the-way page, it is proper to repeat entire this bitter-sweet song of "The Wounded Playmate."

> Half the dreams my spirit hath
> Urge me back on thy lost path,
> Looking for love's aftermath;
>   Aye with some fond gift to share,
> Some light trouble soon o'erthrown;
>   Some old outburst, frank as air,
> Transient as a bugle tone.
>   Angels best can understand
>   How I sometimes miss thy hand
> Yet; and in this indecision
>   For thy footfall pause and pine,
> Beautiful quick-going vision;
>   Unforgotten Soldier mine!
>
> One who knew not pain was dire,
> Trampling out that boyish fire,
> Spurred thy hope with zest entire;
>   Ours what stealth of bow and bat,
> What rash truant oars at sea,
>   Games to last forever, that
> Brake betwixt the child and thee;
>   Many a grudged adventure vast

        Under orchard branches cast;
And at winter's slow dispersal
    (On thy shoulder my hushed mouth),
Scarce allowed, adored rehearsal
    Of the battle-tented South.

Well it was that heaven did give
To a joy so fugitive
Soul, all others to outlive!
    Though to final risks begun
Early exhortation cling;
    Though a sudden deed, ere done,
Lean on thee for sanctioning;
    Though thy knighthood me constrain
    Through age, death, and back again,
Father, most thy memory guiding
    Is a song and star of May;
And the land of thine abiding
    Always Childhood, always Play.

Beyond the Boston of her youth and the Tipperary of her fathers, back to Norfolk in England, where there was a Roger de Geneye, and further on to Marseilles in France, she read her family signposts for those who sought the information. To E. M. Tenison, who has since written a most sympathetic and understanding biography, she wrote:

    There is a great gap, bridged only by tradition: the gap due to the fact that too many of my ancestors, generation after generation, died while their children were very young.

My father only remembered hearing from his father one remark of a genealogical nature: "Cressy was a good battle, Rob, and *we* were in it." Long after he quoted this to me I looked the matter up and found there *was* a Sir Roger Gyney at Cressy, and also his brothers Robert and Thomas, all of Norfolk.

My grandfather Guiney, born in Ireland (husband of a Scots wife Judith Macrae) was far more drawn to Ireland than to any other country, and managed to work "Patrick" into the name of every one of his seven sons, except the youngest who was plain "William." Only two of the seven lived to grow up and marry. The old Gyney or Gueney Christian names, Roger, John, Robert, William, we have never lost.

My grandfather Guiney's grandfather was born in France (near Marseilles) of a French mother, so you see we are rather "mixed" on that side. Holding to the Catholic faith had a lot, almost everything, to do with our getting poorer and poorer. I sold the last acre I owned, in 1910, at the death of my American mother, whose people were Lancashire Holdens and County Carlow Downings and Doyles.

Of her French affiliations, and a racial influence thence, she hints in a letter to Miss Eulalia Geoffrion, who in 1918 was preparing a B.A. thesis on "Louise Imogen Guiney" and had written to the subject for the verification of a bibliography. To give the entire text of the letter is to allow the reader to listen to the author's bantering disregard for much of her own work, much indeed that students of literature, even after our generation, are not going to disregard:

> You couldn't have discovered anyone, I think, who knows less about your subject than I do! I am really ashamed not to be able to help you more. For most of my early work I have a violent dislike, and all my respectable critical work is yet to come. I have four fat books of it accumulating, and nearly ready, having published nothing for eight years. The Muse I have, alas, done with. The Lord gave: the Lord hath taken away.
>
> Your difficulties in getting hold of my Life and Crimes are nothing to be wondered at, as I seem to have murdered every publisher I ever dealt with, Harper and Houghton Mifflin alone excepted. I have not, and never had, a full collection, or anything resembling a collection at all, of my own writings. I am even

under the impression that there is no more of me than your remarkable list would suggest; I greatly admire the energy and industry which it represents!

It gives me peculiar pleasure to hear that you are taking up literary criticism, an art in which our young busy country has been markedly defective. Among Catholics Miss Bregy has almost a monopoly of it, as Miss Repplier, a really great critic, works in a less special field. And here are you, a third French name, in the field! or coming soon into it, which is more than fitting, and entirely racial. Perhaps, if I have any faculty of that kind it is racial, too: for my Irish great-grandfather had a mother born and brought up, and married, near Marseilles.

That constant *pietas* toward her father's kin— "she never ceased to feel a living allegiance to him," wrote Alice Brown out of intimate knowledge— that filial devotion often lit up the aside-glances of her affection. An instance of this wistful eagerness appears in a letter which she wrote from Oxford in 1912 to a Jesuit scholastic shortly before his ordination to the priesthood:

I have to thank you very much, and very specially indeed for the infinitely prized offer to remember me at God's Altar next June. I won't forget the day for which you have thirsted so long. . . .

Sometime, if you know, will you tell me the name, life and crimes of a Father Guiney, S.J., of the Maryland-New York Province. An "S.J." temporarily in Oxford, from California, asked me the other day if I was related. I am almost sure I cannot be, even in a remote degree; but I have so much *pietas* toward my father's all but extinct kin, that I should be interested (on the chance of his being among them) to know a detail or two of Fr. Guiney. Beyond a group of very young first cousins, and some very distant relatives bearing the name, who live, I believe, in Cincinnati (the boys, Edward, George, Robert, were at the Jesuit college there), I fancy I am the only Guiney of that stock. I fear there is no such luck for me as an S.J. namesake.

To the thinning ranks also of her father comrades-in-arms, this *pietas* of pathos and love was communicated; and to observe this loyal regard is to cite here her "Memorial Day":

> O day of roses and regret,
> Kissing the old graves of our own!
> Not to the slain love's lovely debt
> Alone.

The Genearchs of Louise Imogen Guiney 83

> But jealous hearts that live and ache,
> Remember; and while drums are mute,
> Beneath your banners' bright outbreak,
> Salute:
>
> And say for us to lessening ranks
> That keep the memory and pride,
> On whose thinned hair our tears and thanks
> Abide,
>
> Who from their saved Republic pass,
> Glad with the Prince of Peace to dwell:
> *Hail, dearest few! and soon, alas,*
> *Farewell.*

Is it not well to note also that this soldier's daughter was patriot-poet to the last? Though so much of her life was spent abroad—the last ten years amid endeared literary associations and research opportunities in England—exile inspired a great final page. In that volume, *Happy Ending*, which presents her own consummate choice of her poetic work, the precious volume which shows how Catholic and catholic was her genius, Louise Guiney, poet of knight-errantry, must have her exquisite salute to the Flag, for which, as she had once written, her father gave "the unique dual service of Colonel and Color-Bearer." The last page of *Happy Ending* is a sonnet, "In the Docks." (And is there another American "exile" poem like it in any other poet's book?)

> Where the bales thunder till the day is done,
> And the wild sounds with wilder odors cope;
> Where over crouching sail and coiling rope,
> Lascar and Moor along the gangway run;
> Where stifled Thames spreads in the pallid sun,
> A hive of anarchy from slope to slope;
> Flag of my birth, my liberty, my hope,
> I see thee at the masthead, joyous one!
>
> O thou good guest! So oft as, young and warm,
> To the home-wind thy hoisted colors bound,
> Away, away from this too thoughtful ground,
> Sodden with human trespass and despair,
> Thee only, from the desert, from the storm,
> A sick mind follows into Eden air.

But upon the Cross, which is the flag of the soul in all times and latitudes, she set the word *Peace*, and her own heart was in it. Always cheerfully gallant and valorous toward the world of time—in her practical everyday life she unceasingly lived to the letter her galloping song in "The Wild Ride," and her unyielding heart of courage in "The Kings," yet she could describe herself, with "poor lagging man," in "A Footpath Morality," as

> Sick with the impact of mortality;

and again, after play or labor, stand established in an assurance which is deeper than philosophy or poetry,

> Deep in that Will of God, where blend
> The origin of beauty and the end.

It is significant that a Celtic Cross now marks the grave of Louise Imogen Guiney far away in Wolvercote Cemetery, that type of Cross which an old Gaelic world devised for the rest of the world as the symbol of a great truth—a victorious crown firm upon the arms of suffering. She herself set this little monument up in 1903 at the death of her devoted "Aunt Betty" (Elizabeth Doyle); and a note about its details was sent to her devoted friend and co-worker, Miss Gwenllian Morgan:

> I have just had put up a memorial Cross over my dearest Aunty's grave: it is Galway dark gray marble, very slender, and odd simple Celtic pattern which I adapted from an Isle of Man one! It has a rough-hewn base, and two small rough footstones. I think it exceedingly lovely. On the circle, or disc, of the Cross, I have PAX, but no other word on the Cross. Below it, on a table-like smooth surface, in front of the unpolished rock, is the inscription, which I put in Latin for the sake of brevity and the significance not possible in English. . . . The maker, Glanville of Dublin, was indefatigably attentive and intelligent, as I hoped he might be. This gratified me deeply. Thank you, dear, for your

thought of me these anniversary days, with the light upon them of the Will of God.

In the Latin inscription are two words (translated in a marginal note for Miss Morgan) that are now eminently applicable to herself: *In Corde Jesu* (In the Heart of Jesus); *Delassata* (Very weary, or outworn). While one who knew her well, and her filial devotion to her father, might wish that her grave were beside his, a truer consolation sings out that she is with him in the soul-country: *In Corde Jesu.* "It matters not where you bury this body of mine," said Monica to Augustine, saints both; "but remember me when you come to the Altar."

She had written of her father that his memory is altogether wholesome, and where he stands it is clear air. This, too, is the whole world's verdict on the daughter. Of such did Ecclesiasticus (xxx. 4) write over two thousand years ago: The father is dead, and he is as if he were not dead; for he hath left one behind him that is like himself. And to the inspiration of such lives, worthy aspiration of other hearts may read and repeat the happy ending stanza of her "Beati Mortui":

> If thus to have trod and left the wormy way
> Makes men so wondrous gay,
> So stripped and free and potently alive,

The Genearchs of Louise Imogen Guiney 87

Who would not his infirmity survive,
And bathe in victory, and come to be
As blithe as ye,
Saints of the ended wars! Ah, greeting give;
Turn not away, too fugitive:

But hastening toward us, hallow the foul street,
And sit with us at meat,
And of your courtesy, on us unwise
Fix oft those purer eyes,
Till in ourselves who love them dwell
The same sure light ineffable:
Till they who walk with us in after years
Forgetting time and tears
(As we with you), shall sing all day instead:
"How blessed are the Dead."

A MODERN STYLITES

The Old Captain, as the countryside calls him in a loving tone, very graciously allowed me to rehearse in print some notes I gathered in a few precious hours at his mountain oratory. His real name—it is known to countless readers—need not be revealed; and the precise point of the longitude and latitude of his abode may likewise be concealed. It is sufficient to state that he dwells in a compact cottage which is set firmly in a charming dimple of a high hill in Nova Scotia, the hill itself looking firmly and cheerfully north and east, northward across the ingoing Straits of Northumberland, and on clear days saluting eastward the skyline of Cape Breton. If you look thither, he will probably quote a Scripture to you—*mons montem salutat;* for his erudition is prompt with many sentences out of the Book. And if you gaze at the meeting of the waters where the Atlantic takes the Gulf of St. Lawrence, he will add *abyssus abyssum invocat*. And again, if you chance to be his guest on a night of eloquent skies, he will call to witness the truth of an Old Testament sentence: "The stars are called in their watches and they answer, 'Here we are'; and with joy they shine forth to Him that made them." Read in modern literature also, he will add, "Matthew Arnold tried to put that joyous line into his cold poetry."

It is not the air alone, howsoever bracing, that gives him this genial responsiveness and his sparkling eyes. His habitat may well claim a credit page in his book of health; but there are other contributors to that department—his own sane soul being the chief nurse of his sound body. However, he will endeavor to divert your attention from his own wholesome nature and direct your consideration to the inspirational values of the scenes around his abode. "There is the great apothecary shop," he says; and his gesture points out the curative shelves of the obedient skies and the patient hills and the refreshing sea. "A good world, as it was," he began to quote a poem by Louise Imogen Guiney; and when I attempted to misapply a line from Wordsworth, "The world is too much with us," he replied with a genial smile, "Man's misuse of the world is too much with us." And he fell into a dignified protest against the near-sightedness of what he termed the literature of modern Broadways, the skin-deep analyses of Babbitt books and of Gopher Prairie quillists.

From the very first visit I was curious to learn how he came to settle in that remote solitude, like the proverbial sparrow on the housetop, or again, like a Saint Simeon Stylites who went aside from a luxurious society for prayer and penance in a desert. Saints had often refreshed the falling condition of society by their sacrifices; seculars had constantly asserted that a hermitage is salutary—Charles Lamb saying that solitude is the sweet nurse of thought; Bourke Cochrane, that isolation is the price of greatness. From the chaplain at a college four miles away, where I was giving some conferences, I gathered a few fragments about the antecedents of the Old Captain. It was conjectured that he had been an editor and lecturer in the States; that a serious illness had deflected him from his strenuous activities; and now, nearly seventy years of age, having renewed his youth like the eagle, he chose to live on in the environment where he had recuperated his health. I dug out some paragraphs which he contributed to the local diocesan journal during his convalescence; and the editor was pleased to whisper to me that though the *clientèle* of this journal consisted in the main of the simple farmers and fisher-folk of the countryside, yet these paragraphs, being veritable touchstones of thought and criticism, were copied in many newspapers of

A Modern Stylites

America and England, "in the manner of syndicate copy."

The themes of these little essays supplied me with a cue for conversation on the occasions of visit, which indeed were nearly every night; for it was a pleasure to walk the four miles after a day in the academy to have a colloquy with a true academician. If a Londoner, stepping aside from the rain, could detect the learned Edmund Burke after a few minutes of a doorway conversation, one could as promptly conclude that the Old Captain was a man of extensive reading. And if you are adept in diagnosing manners you would readily see that his had been learned in the great school of refinement, namely, patience and resignation; and further still, while some degree of his conversational facility might be attributed to his learning and to his experience and environment, yet he would graciously maintain that he came from a race endowed with readiness of speech; he quoted on one occasion Alice Stopford Green's historical note, "The house of every Irish chieftain in medieval times was an academy of courtesy and conversation."

Though he could invest an argument in the strict logical processes, he seemed to prefer the telling force of an apt illustration. "When one is not in formal controversy," he said, in explanation of his predominant method, "the scene is not set for the driving manner of logic. Then the illustration serves; either conviction follows or silence." And with a knowing smile, he added, "Generally it is silence; for your modern squirms away from conviction. If you pin a conclusion on a cushion of premises, your evading opponent will say aloofly that you are tagging things too insistently."

Growing into his confidence and therefore intimacy as the evenings progressed, I gathered a few of these responses that he made recently to some visitors; for even in that remote countryside travelers occasionally came to his yard—people who, after scanning the scenery from the motor road below, would climb to his shelf on the hill for the wider prospect. "If they have time to rest awhile," he remarked, "they soon turn from these terrestrial horizons to thoughts of deeper and further import —religion, of course. They guess at mine when they notice the crucifix above my porch." And the Old Captain, as I said, permitted me to retell some instances of his replies "to White and Black and Brown," as he named three of the visitors.

"Mr. White," he went on, "an American tourist, was here recently. We had the usual half hour about the vistas by sea and land, and then he angled for a few moments with the hook of religious allu-

A Modern Stylites

sions. The Holy Year became a topic, and I found him enthusiastic about the Brotherhood-of-Man idea as he saw it in this world-wide gathering of pilgrims in the Eternal City. He had enthusiasms on other Catholic topics; and his tone was sincere as he thanked me for some answers to his questions, answers that contained after all only the elements of our teaching. As he went down the hill late that evening, he turned for a few moments in solemn silence, and then made ejaculations about the sublimity of the Catholic Church, about its fullness, its response to all the appeals of the human heart and life; then, strange to relate, he added with dramatic intensity, 'I think I would be a Catholic only for the fact that there are so many millions of Catholics who know little or nothing about their great religion.' "

The Old Captain knew the art of pausing, though the listener be intent. "I began to tell him," he went on, "that nearly every parish sermon urges on Catholics the need of knowing their holy religion more fully, when suddenly I turned to a parallel for a response. In the late war, said I, we had millions of American men under arms, a million or perhaps more already in the trenches, ready and earnest to die in their country's cause; and they were right to be willing to make that sacrifice of their lives. Yet of that vast army not fifty thousand knew the Constitution of the United States, knew even the Declaration of Independence, nor the history of the Stars and Stripes. But—they knew their country. . . . I did not need to urge the parallel. . . . His eyes told me that he saw the point. He pressed my hand warmly and went away in silence, realizing, I think, that the millions of Catholics know and love and obey the One, Holy, Catholic, Apostolic Church though they have not read its theology nor mastered the ritual."

Another American tourist was Mr. Black. "He came this way from a New England city during the war, having a two weeks' furlough from a training camp. It was not long before he touched upon religion, anxious, as he said, to get the Catholic viewpoint, as he was engaged to a Catholic girl. We drifted about for some minutes on the borders, so to speak; then I asked him if he could give me a starting point in his own beliefs, some fundamental tenets that he held. He gave a few vague and indefinite statements that he remembered from lectures under Professor Royce. . . . I tried another method of arrival: I asked him to state very candidly some Catholic doctrine or practice which tended to jar him in his attitude toward the Church. His reply was quick and definite; it con-

A Modern Stylites

cerned the Index—your Index of prohibited books, he said; why not allow people to judge for themselves whether the book be worthy or not, error or truth."

"You yourself, said I, after a moment, play the Index in your home. For let me suppose that you have a young sister and brother; you would not allow a salacious book or magazine on their table. He admitted that, and he was silent. . . . Now, I had clipped but a few days before a newspaper note from a journal of his own New England city; it had material for a serviceable illustration. In your native city, I said, citizens were selected recently to examine the books in the public library, to withdraw such books as seemed to favor the enemy and such as might possibly be harmful to American ideals; and the volumes thus withdrawn were publicly burned in the library yard. . . . Now, according to your theory, these books should have been allowed to remain on the shelves; and young Americans, let us say, boys and girls from the high schools, should have been permitted to read the books and decide for themselves if these writings were detrimental and subversive of American doctrine and ideals. But the sane and judicious mind of the community decided otherwise. . . . And the Church, which is always at war with two great

enemies, error and vice, always maintaining aloft
the banner of truth and virtue, appoints her judicious committee. . . . Hence the Index. . . . I
could proceed no further, for he gave a significant
gesture. That was his starting point—four years
ago. He writes me that he is coming to see me . . .
the week before his entrance to the Church."

The story about Mr. Brown also had a sequel.
"He first came here in a yacht, on his wedding tour,
as I learned. He was anchored in the cove down
there, and one calm evening he climbed up here
and seemed entranced with the vista and the redolence from the fields and forests. He quickly caught
sight of the crucifix above my porch, and without
any hesitation, told me that his wife was Catholic.
Immediately I saw a shade of pain come across his
features. I quickly averted my glance and thought
to continue upon the theme of the landscape. But he
would not delay with the burden of his heart, with
his cause of sorrow. His wife was a Catholic, he
repeated; but they were not married according to
her law, that is, before a priest. And as he went
on, I was amazed at his telling me the history so
directly, and at no query on my part. He was
deeply concerned about his wife. He wanted to see
her happier. . . . Could I, he asked, suggest how
his wife could go to the Sacraments. . . . Perhaps

I knew some priest, or perhaps still the Bishop. . . . How could his wife be admitted again to the Sacraments of her Church?"

The Old Captain chose to pause here before he resumed: he pretended to point toward the cove where the yacht had been. "I gently asked him why the marriage had not been according to the Catholic ritual. . . . Because he would not sign the papers to have all the children educated in his wife's religion; he would agree to let the girls go with the mother, but the boys should have his religion. Now first of all I had a certain admiration for him; for here was a doctor, hoping to have children, and a gentleman who was honorably worried over his wife's religious condition. After a difficult silence, I asked him why he would not sign the papers to allow all the children to be brought up in his wife's religion; and he replied quite firmly that to do so would be against his conscience. That again was honorable ground to stand upon; and though I could have touched upon his lack of consistency and of logic in the situation, I met his response at a different angle. Your conscience, Doctor: I honor you there. But let me ask you, very kindly I ask you, why you allowed a girl to whom you professed love and loyalty to go against her conscience. You, her lover and chivalrous knight, should have prevented her from violating her conscience, as she did when she attempted to marry outside the rules of her Church."

Later in the evening I learned that Mr. Brown had returned on the following day to tell the Old Captain that his wife had been admitted to the Sacraments. And when I went back to my college room I found an old-fashioned spyglass which enabled me to scan the far horizons. Focusing the lens, I picked out the house of the Old Captain. In that line of vision it looked like a figure on a cylindrical shaft, not now as when the visitor faces it from the road below and sees it framed in a shelf-like cranny. For the minute I recalled the old hermits who went into solitude, away from the noisy sciences and industrialisms and sensual pleasures of their day, and who discoursed to the multitudes about penance and prayer. "What went ye out in the desert to see!" I looked steadily and I saw a lamp light at the Old Captain's sanctuary on the mountain shaft. Then I reviewed a paragraph which he had written in the diocesan journal on a text from the Gospel: "The light of thy body is the eye. If thy eye be single, thy whole body will be lightsome; but if it be evil, thy body also will be darksome. . . . What a text for poet and sage!"

his editorial began; and it was followed by another meditation on a poet's couplet:

> These to whom the heavens must ope,—
> Candor, Chastity and Hope.

Perhaps I shall return to the Old Captain on the summit and ask him about some of the current fads that perplex a sick world—psychoanalysis, for one of them. Surely he will smile and allude to the defunct fads of other days, the skin-deep sciences of palmistry, of craniology, and other pseudo-diagnoses on character and temperament and temptation and trial. Doubtless he will prove that true psychoanalysis may find its curative formulas in the Gospel, in the Epistles of St. Paul, in the à Kempis book of the *Imitation;* for he knows the score of texts that assert in what things a man shall sow in those shall he reap: and again, *in patientia vestra possidebitis animas vestras.*

FATHER SHEALY

It is something to be a notable figure on a college campus, to be revered for high qualities of mind and heart by the students of the day and acclaimed by them in graduate reminiscences three or four generations later; and it is more unique to present that same notableness on a civic campus—the plaza, for instance, that faces New York City Hall, and the purlieus thereof. Father Terence J. Shealy, S.J., achieved that fame both as a college professor and as a master of retreats. At Holy Cross, where he was teacher of rhetoric thirty years ago, he was the outstanding figure of student praise; a Scholastic—the name to designate his *status* before priesthood—he seemed to his classes and sodalities the modern embodiment of that medieval and university title; and when he came out upon the terraces after classes, faces would turn from games, and voices would whisper, "There's Shealy"; and twenty-five years later, one of those classes, preparing a Commencement reunion, earnestly petitioned him to come back to Holy Cross for their honor and homage. Fordham and Georgetown

Father Shealy

may speak, perhaps in higher tones, this page about him. Upon a larger campus, in that other department of his life work, the retreat movement, especially in its New York center, esteem shone out from the very start—for his zeal, his mentality, his character, in a word, his personality. "I merely want to look at him again," said an unsentimental, practical business man from up-State five hours after he had come from Manresa; "I do not want to take any of his valuable time, but I must get a look at him again before I leave town." Similar enthusiasm may be heard if one listens in on the conversations of thousands of his retreatants today. Witness this refrain from one recently advanced to a judgeship in the Supreme Court of New York: "I wish my mother and Father Shealy were here to share the honor." His memory is in clear and assured places; his disciples—that is their chosen name—have enshrined his name magnificently in the Father Shealy Memorial Building; and though he may not enter poetic eulogy as a lamented Thyrsis or Lycidas, the men of the street have already their singing sincerity around his name:

> Now, Shealy of the Jesuits
>   Was a great man in his day;
> He taught the youngsters in the school,
>   And taught us men to pray;
> He put his mind to higher points

That few can understand,
But Shealy of the Jesuits
Gave common men his hand.

Now this Jesuit of America was born in Ireland, April 30, 1863. American in the fruitful labors of his lifetime—what teacher insisted more eloquently on the worth of American principles?— and alert as any Martial in cosmopolitan interest for mankind—*Homo sum et nihil humanum alienum a me puto*—he retained through all his years the exquisite presentation of the best in Munster culture. His childhood looked well upon the noble landscape and environs of Galteemore, near Mitchelstown in the County Cork. His early years of study met with the attention of the distinguished Canon Peter O'Leary, whom Gaelic scholars call the acknowledged master of modern Irish prose, and, let us add, O'Leary's own inspiring preceptor in his own youth had been the great Archbishop MacHale. The young Shealy does not appear to have had an opportunity to follow the Gaelic studies of the master or the grand-master,— the foster-fathers, as they would be called in Gaelic. He very probably revealed at an early age his desire to serve God at the altar; for when Canon O'Leary departed from Mitchelstown for another parish, he guided his young protégé to a Latin school in the new district. To the venerable Canon and the school Father Shealy sped with filial memory when he returned to Ireland twenty years later for the final year of his theological studies. If his visit did not mark him as an adept in the language and lore of ancient Ireland, his eyes and heart bespoke his zeal for young America; if the body of the old land was only fragmentary knowledge to him, he comprehended her soul, entire and intimate, for its vitalizing service to the new world. His message to his classes, whether academic or communal, was to be not in terms of the body's profit and gain, but in the ideals of the soul, in the ideals from the Mount of Beatitudes: baptized and nurtured in the national faith of his great motherland, he would call his new country to keep "this terrible and splendid trust, this heritage of the race of kings," this selfsame lure of God in its eyes and heart. "There is more in Erin's heart than Tom Moore ever sang to the chords of his gentle harp," he once dictated to a young Sophomore at Holy Cross; and further: "There is more meaning clustered around her ivy-clad round towers, her picturesque abbeys, her storied valleys and green hills than would immortalize the names of more than a dozen Scotts." And to that same pupil, touring in Ireland after graduation, Father Shealy wrote: "Sit on the back seat of the coach, and see the old land receding from you, and feel the beauty and the glory of its past; it is the land of the past; God knows its future." The light in Columcille's "gray eye," when that great scholar-saint moved to exile, was ever in Father Shealy's own of dark blue. Indeed he is worthily named in the long line that has come out of the island of saints and scholars, of the clan of Columcille and Columbanus, of Archbishop MacHale and Canon O'Leary; and Holy Cross in Worcester and Manresa in New York, as witnesses to his life and work, are ready to appreciate the glorious records which history retains about the scholar-saints of Iona in the north of Europe and of Bobbio in the south.

Again, besides the influence of his early countryside and school, the inspiration of his home and mother was a vitalizing force through all his life. The memory of these sacred objects ran like a golden thread, a wholesome interlinear, through much of his thought and language, through he was not speaking to be overheard or under-read. His classes caught "the feel of it" many a time when he commented on some classic text, or threw out a theme for consideration in verse, or paused to wish them a merry Christmas. His former pupils remember the day "the great Ted" exulted in a

Father Shealy

commentary over a phrase of Tacitus—that relation of the educational source of Agricola's greatness, *sinu indulgentiaque matris*, at the loving heart of a mother. And the men of Manresa can recall the exaltation of this idea in a thousand utterances from Father Shealy: "The Lord, to reform the world and the home, began with the cradle. He went down into the womb of life and blessed it there, gave it a home and mother; and through this home and mother He would renew the face of the earth."

The glorification of that theme—a memory of his own mother—sparkled in his oratory; but it is a shining and steady light in one great poem that he wrote, a poem, sad to relate, which is given in no anthology of Catholic or American or Irish poetry, though it is in many a "scrapbook" in the four corners of the world. And, if I may be pardoned the injection of a pronoun in the first person, I have read this poem in a lecture on "Exile Poetry" to over seventy thousand people, and know well how it sways the tender emotions of the audience, whatever the age of the hearers, young or old, or their racial origins, Slav or Teuton, Latin and Celtic, Americans all. Being asked by Stopford Brooke and T. W. Rolleston to collect the Anglo-Irish poetry of our country, I quickly forwarded the two poems by Father Shealy, written at the time of his ordination to the priesthood: "From My Mother in Ireland," and "To My Mother in Ireland." Stopford Brooke replied: "This is true poetry, great poetry—the first one, I mean; the second seems inferior. Indeed it is hard to believe that they were written by the same hand." And a similar estimate of these poems was made by their author. For when I expressed a proposal of republishing the two pieces, he wrote: "I have no copy of the Ode (the second piece named above) and should prefer you would not publish it with the Ballad (the first named). It needs revising; I was never satisfied with it. I may do the revising in some favorable mood, and then forward it to you." But, alas, the re-created Ode never came. "I am at fever heat in the retreat work," he would write, "the great Apostolate of the hour, and can find time for nothing else at present." That present was unbroken, his laborious yesterdays and tomorrows in his *indivisible nunc*. Yet he longed to participate in the Apostolate of the pen; to the dictum made famous by Fletcher of Saltoun and Daniel O'Connell, he made an insistent appeal: Give me the making of a nation's ballads and I care not who makes its laws. "The song that fires a nation's heart is in itself a deed," he said insist-

Father Shealy

ently. And, since his legion of admirers will admit any fragment of his letters, I cite his aspirations in a note anent a little book of mine:

> It was a joy to my eyes and heart to see your name to it, and I say to you most warmly, "more power to your pen and brain" . . . Your hands, as Canon Sheehan's, will do great things for Faith and Country. . . . I should love to have a little leisure to put in form some ambitions of my own. Alas! dreams, dreams, and stern facts are pressing all around. . . . Pray for me and the great retreat work.

But, omitting for the present a word about three dramas which he wrote in his Scholastic days, and returning to that topic of a lifelong inspiration, his mother and home, let us agree that he wrote one great poem of abiding memory: "From My Mother in Ireland; for my First Mass." Here is the theme and the Parnassus of all great poetry, ancient and modern: *pro aris et focis*. And awaiting the anthology that is to contain it, harken to these "snatches" of his song:

> The joy is come, *alanna*,
> That I watched for through the years;
> And my heart is full of blessing,
> But my eyes are full of tears:

The joy is come, *alanna,*
And I am far away—
The mother will not see her boy,
Upon his first Mass day.

* * *

Enough, enough, to breathe my name
When Christ is in your hand—
Oh, don't forget your father's grave
And poor old Ireland.

* * *

I've placed the flowers and candles
For the Mass that might have been,
But my eyes, *agra,* can't find their rest,
My joy is all within.

* * *

I'll wait for you at morn,
And I'll pray with you till noon,
And every eve I'll dream of you,
My own *Soggarth aroon.*

From the altar in Woodstock, the first offerings of his "spiritual bouquet" were transmitted to the cottage at home, and the first also of the material remembrances from that altar—the white linen bands that were wound about his fingers at the ordination:

These blessed gifts I wrapped with care,
Fragrant with the breath of prayer,
  In this little linen strip—
  Press it sweetly to thy lip:
Lady, lady, 'tis the band
Tied thy child's anointed hand.

Father Shealy

The last Mass Father Shealy said in Ireland was in his mother's cottage. She was of the race of saints; and when her son turned to give the *Benedicat vos* at the end of Mass, behold; the mother knelt before him, holding up her burial shroud for that blessing. It was her beautiful solace and heroic readiness against a distant day.

From this heart and hearth, when he was seventeen years of age, he proceeded for further studies to the famous Apostolic College, at Mungret, near Limerick. The school and its environs are located in a center of glorious traditions, a sacred soil where an older Mungret enacted scenes of learning and holiness. Even the modern Apostolic College, young yet in its history, is already a rich confessor of its faith and scholarship, having consummated much in a brief space, an Alma Mater indeed for the *Sancta Mater Ecclesia* in all parts of the world, with a record that merits the pen of a Joseph Farrell to write it parallel to his chapter on *Les Missions Etrangères, Paris*. Colleges and parishes in the United States know alumni of Mungret, three of whom out of its yesterday are Bishops and one an Archbishop. Within its studious halls, the young Shealy developed that ripe and solid character for scholarship and piety which marked him everywhere afterwards; and his cultural evaluation of historical vestiges and literary landmarks called out paths for his holiday walks. It was not a great distance to reach footprints of Sarsfield, or to cross Thomond Bridge and meditate near the broken stone of the Broken Treaty.

> But oftener did we muse along those ways
> Thought-laden with the glory of our dead;
> Where Thomond and the perjured Treaty Stone
> And Sarsfield's lofty spirit still survive:
> While old Saint Mary's bells their silver notes
> Send forth from out the flood.
> And oft we mused
> Mid every broken arch and rent of ruin
> That mark in Limerick's ancient battlements
> The Saxon tread, that with'ring tread of worse
> Than Danish hordes,— the tread of Strongbow's men,
> The tread that's burnt deep into our plains.

Adare was no great distance—O, sweet Adare! of Gerald Griffin's song, "the soft retreat of sylvan splendor." And Aubrey de Vere had his abode there in Shealy's school-days.

> Now, where the list'ning groves of Curraghchase
> Away amid the peasant roofs enjoy
> The purest voice in all the choir of song
> Within our time, the Voice of Eire's Faith,
> Her golden years—her sainted ones of yore—
> Too great to catch the tawdry modern sense,—
> De Vere, the singer unto nobler days.

The B.A. of the Royal University of Ireland—

Father Shealy

how his friends pleasantly bantered him about it in American years!—awaited him at the end of his Mungret studies; there was no banter about his desserts in regard of that or a higher degree. He returned to teach at his Alma Mater for one year; then on September 4, 1886, he entered the old Jesuit novitiate at Frederick, Maryland. Within those humble walls he cultivated and enlarged that ascetical spirit which was the basis of his genius in giving retreats; and in the acres outside, his love of traditions could meet with objects—in the yard was the inscribed stone above the grave of Roger Brooke Taney, and in a cemetery nearby the cenotaph of Francis Scott Key, Taney's brother-in-law; and the clustered spires of Frederick, and the valley rich with corn, green-walled by the hills of Maryland, as Whittier related, looked pleasantly on the Catoctin Mountains: "for all the world like the Wicklow Hills," Father Shealy wrote in a letter fifteen years later. Thence he passed on to his studies at Woodstock, then as a Scholastic teacher at Fordham and Holy Cross; again back at Woodstock for his theological studies—the fourth year being at Milltown Park in Ireland—and, final in the course, his Tertianship at Florissant, Missouri. The discipline of Scholastic philosophy and theology found in him a mind pliable and acute, but his heart preferred the patristic literature, "those great minds and mines of the Fathers," he said, exhorting a Montreal seminarian. He knew his Chrysostom and Augustine, not their matter only, but their form; the force and fire of the Greek Father and the brilliant antitheses of the Latin were captive in his own oratory and captivated his audiences.

If I may venture to state a comparison with a modern in sacred oratory, I would say that his pulpit is alongside of the famous Lacordaire's. In the cogent sequences of logic and impounded argument, in the brilliant flashes of rhetorical fire, and in the gothic grandeur which he erected around a proposition on the Kingdom of God, he is on a plane with the renowned Dominican, though the latter, as we may conjecture, was more attentive to the effectiveness of elocution. Again, on the score of written style—"the crucifixion of the pen," as Lacordaire termed that labor—the French orator zealously took time to preserve for the eye the conferences which delighted and captivated the ears of Notre Dame. Father Shealy lacked the opportunity to elaborate his transcriptions. His genius is to be perceived in notes or in shorthand reports of his discourses; yet even in this form they are pages that deserve to be cherished.

Take a paragraph at random from a stenogra-

Father Shealy

pher's transcript: extempore, yet how coherent and forceful in matter and form, in the oratorical climax that goes from the human soul to the Heart of Christ and on again to the soul of man:

> In this world of ours we have changed the horizon of the soul of man. All our perspectives and values are changed; we would find a new center of gravity for life. We are trying to find a new standard in matter, and we are bankrupt in the midst of inventions and triumphs. We are sick at heart: we are in the midst of distress, distrust and conflict. We are submerged by over-reaching competition and jobbery, by strange values and valuations. Yet when we turn to the Gospel we find that there is one central thought running through it all; and that thought centers in the sacredness of human life. If there is one mark in the Gospel it is the emphasis of this individualization. The reform of the soul through Christ the Lord is the soul of all reform; and He would renew the heart and spirit of man, and through that heart and spirit renew the face of the earth. And therefore, the question of our time, the central question of all time, is not the political question; it is not the industrial question; it is not the social ques-

tion: under whatever aspect you conceive it, it is in its last analysis an ethical question. For there is not a human act that has not an ethical value. This is the one power on which the great Reformer, the great Civilizer, the great Educator, the great Liberator, Christ the Lord, centered His vision, centered His education—the soul and heart of man.

Out of the multitude of voices, old and young, that have acclaimed his pulpit, one in particular is a pleasant reminiscence to give. Father Edward Purbrick—*quantus qualisque vir atque sacerdos!*—who had been a beloved disciple of Newman and Oxford, was Visitor and Provincial to the Maryland-New York Province twenty-five years ago, and during a visit to Woodstock he was witness to the thrill of the young theologian's oratory. The occasion was the inconsiderate hour of noonday dinner, and Mr. Shealy in his turn at a sermon; and Father Purbrick told me three years later, "I still remember the brilliant sermon he preached in Woodstock, and though I had to make a pretence at eating, in reality I did nothing but listen, spellbound by the thought and manner." Going from this Scholasticate as priest and teacher to Georgetown, his course of Advent sermons in Trinity Church marked him for the pulpit, though the

Father Shealy

classroom wanted him; and before his Tertianship and his appointment to New York and the laymen's league that was to follow, he proved his power as a retreat-giver before worthy communities. Affectionate memory attests this statement among the Visitation nuns at Georgetown (his name is in the daily prayer there), the Carmelites at Roxbury, the Notre Dame Sisters at Trinity College, and at Marymount on the Hudson.

Marymount and Father Shealy is an ample volume of lectures and conferences which he delivered to the nuns and students of the college—a glorious witness to his devoted zeal and his untiring apostleship.

But before we bring him to his New York base, let us return to his Scholastic days when he was in the classroom, first at Fordham and then at Holy Cross. Of the period at Fordham reminiscent voices might contribute a glowing hour in his regard; he was a stimulating mentor, both in and out of the classroom, to many there; *crede experto,* Martin H. Glynn had an earnest bench in that class on his way to a seat in Congress and the chair of Governor in New York. But at Holy Cross the remembered record is fuller and nearer at hand. Mr. Shealy's "regency" there in the mid-nineties was part of the inception of a new growth and vigor in the life of the college. The huge O'Kane building, forerunner of five ampler buildings since erected, was at its foundation. Father Hanselman, in the Office of Studies, was adding to a richer scholarship among the students a spirit of social democracy which is even today the characteristic of "the City on the Hill." Among the Faculty, Father McLaughlin in the department of philosophy, Father Dufour in French, Father Jones in dramatics and public speaking were names to be signaled, are names cherished by many; so speak Senator David I. Walsh and Judge John P. O'Brien, and others in that cloud of witnesses. In this group stood, and stood highest, the Scholastic Shealy. To his classes he was more than an encyclopedia and a voice: he was an oracle of interpretation of classic literature, ancient and modern, of great events in history, and of present-day issues. He was a master humanist— where is there a Justin McCarthy or a Henry Adams to relate that of him adequately? He was an inspiration whether he was placing a book in a student's hands or a message in his heart. And his classes produced books, the first that came out of Holy Cross as yearbooks: *Acroama* by the class of '95, and *Eutropius* of '96. The College Journal, *The Purple,* had his direction in its first two years with essays and verse that still deserve reading; and,

Father Shealy

to add a word about the distinctive typography and make-up, Father Edward Welch used to bring the monthly issues into his post-graduate classes in Georgetown to deliver his exquisite praise on the exquisite appearance of *The Purple* page. In that renaissance of literary activities at that period in Holy Cross, Shealy paid a glorious *Vale* to an old stage, and a more glorious *Ave* to a new one. His Latin play, *Sybylla*, presented by his Worcester sodalities, was the last performance on "the boards" of the old Fenwick Hall; and his magical pen wrote a Greek drama, *Eutropius*, which his class presented at the opening of the new Fenwick. The *Sybylla* received its deserving *Vos plaudite*. Based upon an old Gaelic legend, its flowing Latin narrative and choral odes told the story of the quest of Gaelic sibylline books for the Messiah. And *Eutropius*, which has its motivation in the tyranny of the infamous prime minister in the Constantinople of Arcadius, gave rhetoric and history a splendid setting for the famous oration of St. John Chrysostom over the fallen Eutropius. In its praise a Greek column appeared in *Atalantis*, and a Greek consul sent a jubilant note to his office in Athens.

After leaving Holy Cross, he wrote another drama the following year in the free-times from study at Woodstock. It was in English, upon a theme and scenes in modern Ireland; in it Irish ideals and endeavor played their parts and a sunburst of hope lit up the eventual landscape—fiber of that golden thread which runs through all true poetry of the Gael—'Tis morn upon the hills of Inisfall. I had the privilege of visiting him at Woodstock and was confidentially entrusted with the manuscript. An amateurish critique went back with it; and "It's resting in my trunk" was the only word I heard of it three years later. But Father Shealy's tendency to go to drama with his message is significant; it displays a literary characteristic racial in the Gael, since Ireland is the origin of the dramatic element even in English letters—a claim that is easy to find in the pages of the Irish Douglas Hyde, the English-Irish Stopford Brooke and the French Jules Jusserand.

Though the romantic prettinesses of the Rosa Mulholland novels in those nineties were dear to his eyes, dearer to his heart was the insight, already Sinn Fein, in the ballads of Dora Sigerson. He knew the causes why the Irish Cause never dies—one of them:

> The Brehon Law of Ireland! Those laws were splendid in symmetry and proportion, magnificent in the treatment of rights and duties, and especially on the question of

Father Shealy

woman's position in the home and in society. And that is the test in any civilization. Then England came along; and England acted the tyrant more by depriving the Irish of their language and customs and their laws than by robbing them of their fields and firesides. There is no robbery equal to that. They may burn my home before my very eyes and confiscate my lands around me, and yet life remains individual and personal and natural. But the moment they impose a foreign life upon me, impose a foreign language and foreign customs upon me, that moment they put the rope around my neck, my heart and my soul. That is one wrong England has done to Ireland.

And had Father Shealy remained in Ireland— well, intellectuals from his circle would have fallen in 1916, as Thomas MacDonough and Joseph Mary Plunkett fell, whose art and ethics seem to have come out of his classroom.

But his classrooms were to be for America and for the Kingdom of God. New York with the twentieth century became his oratory and laboratory. He had groups for philosophy at St. Xavier College, and later for jurisprudence at Fordham, and larger audiences betimes before him in the pulpit and the platform. But in 1909 he set his stage for the great drama of the retreat movement: that Play was the thing to capture consciences for the King. What magical phrases invested his inspiring appeals for "this stock-taking in matters pertaining to man's destiny!" And still the wonder grew, and by 1911 his ardent followers enabled him to purchase a fixed abode for the laymen's retreats, "a spiritual Country Club," Manresa on Staten Island. From this American Iona he carried the lay apostolate to Harrisburg and Emmittsburg, to Atlantic City, Oswego, Springfield, Massachusetts, and Hartford, Connecticut, and to Albany and Washington; and Philadelphia owns now a permanent house after his labors at Overbrook. His grateful followers are erecting the magnificent Father Shealy Memorial Building at Manresa, a monument of memory to him and a service for the work that was his zeal. Well begun, the campaign is already half done; "what Father Shealy wished it to be," wrote Mr. Fitzsimmons, the League's President, "a place where men shall come in evergrowing numbers to renew their strength that they may better fight the good fight for God."

His memory is likewise a keepsake in the hearts of thousands, thousands literally; for during his last year over two thousand men attended his New

Father Shealy

York retreats. Consult their notes, some of them made *in extenso* at his conferences and all indelibly stamped upon their resolutions. Take this one: "*Parati sunt aut vivere aut mori fortiter*—They were prepared to live or die bravely, undauntedly, gallantly, generously. We have no word in English for the Latin *fortiter,* but any one of these words will come very near its meaning. Religion is the great spiriting, the great inspiring force. No man lives *fortiter* who is a coward in thought. One may be a Knight of Columbus or a Holy Name man and be a sham. These titles mean nothing unless one lives up to one's Christian manhood. A great deal is expected from every Catholic man, from every Catholic layman. He is expected to stand up for his country, his Church, his religion, whenever circumstances call for his assistance. Where is the ambition of our Catholic laymen for the honor and reverence of the religion he professes? There are few, too few, active, energetic Catholic laymen to defend the cause of God and His Church. Let our Catholic men take this to heart. Let them think *fortiter,* will *fortiter,* live *fortiter*—put ye on the Lord Christ."

This was his slogan, not a mere catch-phrase—manhood for life, manhood for Christ. His spiritual psychology called for minds that were frank, candid, honest; for wills prompt to obey, easily subjected to discipline; and for hearts that would inspire personal enthusiasm, unselfish devotion, and be the effective source for patriotism and fidelity to God. His public orations carried the same message.

And therefore his epitaph is manifold. A business man who was accustomed to follow him about and take his addresses in shorthand and then transcribe them in a busy office the next day, added this footnote to one set of discourses; and men of Manresa will not think it over-enthusiastic: "Father Shealy is a great American, a great Irish man, a great orator, a great philosopher, a great patriot, a great saint! God be praised!"

THE SERVICE OF THE VOICE

The pen is very active about the voice in our present educational efforts. What a plethora of textbooks carry their ephemeral circulation on the topic of public speaking! What manuals of promise for singers and orators! The "movies" print imaginary voices and must be content with a whirlwind of gesticulation and the pitiable display of facial gymnastics. Radio audiences, on the other hand, cannot look for the dignified acting of an Edwin Booth, nor the artistry in gesture of a Wendell Phillips. And, in the realms of oratory and song, many of us, like the poet, "look before and after, and pine for what is not." With sane regret we are allowed to look across to recent yesterdays and marvel at the triumphs of Jenny Lind and Adelina Patti, and at the splendors in other scenes of the Daniels—Webster and O'Connell.

Consider for a moment the marvelous voice of Bossuet, and the brilliant paragraph which Lamartine set around it. Yet it is not the mere voice which is eulogized—declamatory excellence, vacuous of thought—*vox et praeterea nihil*. Bossuet's elocution was magnificent because his message, both in thought and application, was magnificently organized and charged with authority. Lamartine adequately reveals that in his grand period:

> What a voice! A voice which is never hoarse, broken, soured, irritated or troubled by the worldly and passionate struggles of interest peculiar to the time: a voice which, like that of the thunder in the clouds, or the organ in the cathedral, has never been anything but the medium of power and divine persuasion to the soul: a voice which speaks only to kneeling auditors: a voice which is listened to in profound silence, to which none reply save by an inclination of the head or by falling tears—those mute applauses of the soul: a voice which is never refuted or contradicted, even when it astonishes or wounds; a voice, in fine, which does not speak in the name of opinion, which is variable; nor in the name of philosophy, which is open to discussion; nor in the name of country, which is local; nor in the name of legal supremacy, which is temporal; nor in the name of the speaker himself, who is an agent transformed for the occasion: but which speaks in the name of God—an authority of language unequaled

The Service of the Voice

upon earth, and against which the lowest murmur is impious and the smallest opposition a blasphemy.

Bossuet, then, as the schools admit, possessed the full philosophy of oratory; he had educated his mind and heart deeply before he achieved skill in declamation for his voice. "Preaching is thinking aloud for God," said Cardinal Manning; "let your mind and heart work." And when this first requisite is attained, when profound preliminaries in study have been made, how glorious and glorifying is the service of the voice. Elocution then wears the aureole of art; and the voice becomes endowed with greater reaches in tonality, with richer capabilities in enunciation; it is a glorified handmaid to other arts. Lamartine's paragraph explains how Bossuet's voice labored as a devoted and skilful servant for his rhetoric, for his theology and asceticism, and for the Name in which he spoke. Who, even if his auditory delight were less than Lamartine's, would not wish to hear Bossuet in one of his sublime symphonies of speech, were it only for the space of a paragraph such as this from the "Funeral Oration on Henrietta of France":

> Christians, ye who have been called from all sides to this ceremony by the memory of a great Queen—daughter, wife, mother of

powerful kings and of sovereigns of three kingdoms—this discourse will bring before you one of those conspicuous examples which spread before the eyes of the world its absolute vanity. You will see in a single life all the extremes of human affairs: boundless felicity and boundless misery; a long and peaceful possession of one of the world's noblest crowns; all that can be given of the glories of birth and rank gathered upon a head which is afterwards exposed to all the insults of fortune; the good cause at first rewarded by success, then met by sudden turns and unheard-of changes; rebellion long restrained, at last over-riding everything; unbridled licentiousness; the destruction of all laws; royal majesty insulted by crimes before unknown; usurpation and tyranny under the name of liberty; a queen pursued by her enemies, and finding no refuge in either of her kingdoms; her own native land become a melancholy place of exile; many voyages across the sea undertaken by a princess, in spite of the tempest; the ocean surprised at being crossed so often, in such different ways, and for causes so different; a throne shamefully destroyed and miraculously restored. Those are the lessons

The Service of the Voice

which are given by God to the kings; thus does He show to the world the emptiness of its pomps and splendors. If I lack words, if expression is unable to do justice to a subject of such magnitude and loftiness, things alone will speak sufficiently; the heart of a great queen, formerly raised by long years of prosperity and suddenly plunged into an abyss of bitterness, will speak loudly enough; and if private characters are not allowed to give lessons to princes upon such strange occurrences, a king lends me his voice to tell them: *Et nunc, reges, intelligite; erudimini, qui judicatis terram:* Understand now, ye kings of the earth; learn, ye who judge the world.

Voice, let us reiterate, is a handmaid to the art of oratory, even as lights and shadows are to the painter and to the artist in stained glass. And voice enters with supreme service into other realms of letters, to the art of poetry especially. This observation needs not emphatic insistence; for all the world admits that good reading is a lost art nowadays, and that, in consequence, the magical productions of lyrical poetry too often suffer a mute, inglorious sepulture. Excellent lyrics, which bear tidings of a beautiful message and wear the vesture of fine craftsmanship, are read with sealed lips—

the eye, perhaps, finding a silent appeal, but the ear deaf to sweet rhythms and assonances. Poetry ought not to be a dead language; it deserves more than the semi-consciousness which attends it. And yet it is only semi-possessed of vitality when it is read in the lipless fashion of our day, or, what is worse, with our ineptitudes of drawl and tonelessness.

It is not far to find a splendid illustration of a voice which serves as a faithful acolyte in the sanctuary of poetry, a voice in song akin to Bossuet's in oratory, though it lack a Lamartine for eulogist. We are not citing Mr. John McCormack for scientific displays in the grand realms of opera and oratorio, neither are we focusing him in comparison with vocal masters in our past quarter of a century; we bring him forward here in the academy as an ideal reader of lyrical and ballad poetry, as an artist whose voice has done eminent service in a department of letters, making the lyric and ballad stand out in high relief. The critics of the musical world have exhausted praise of him and stamped with popular approbation their superlatives about his accomplished performances—his tonal richness, his flawless technique, his interpretative power in varied genres of structure, whether with an aria by Handel or Mozart, with a medieval mode in Irish music,

The Service of the Voice

the haunting rhythm of a song by some worthy modern, or a wholesome ballad that has reached the hearts of the people.

Literature, therefore, as well as music, has the right and privilege to greet him. Balladists and the makers of lyrics hold him a powerful ally, a craftsman in co-operation, a fortunate partner to have, lifting their silent lines out of the dumb page, and setting them with full understanding and feeling in the hearts of all who come within the range of his voice. His song recitals are lectures in poetry interpretations; though renowned in the musical science, he is a supreme interpreter in his field of literature. A mere voice could not merit that eloquence. But, as Bossuet possessed the philosophy of oratory, so McCormack knows the philosophy of song: Bossuet spoke in the name of God; McCormack sings in the intelligence of the human heart. Intellectual processes and humanistic appraisals precede his recitations; for if his reading of poetry through the medium of song were merely a matter of heart, the effect would arrive only in emotionalism and sentimentalism. As in Bossuet's training the mastery of resourceful sciences became the foundation of oratorical perfection, so the student's zeal over the text which he is to sing is the basis of McCormack's power in vocal interpretations. Educated in schools where humanistic valuations put a vesture of worth upon the true literature of the classroom, he carries the precepts of college days into perfect practice on the public platform. Erudition remembers for him how prominent was the part which choral odes played in old Greek tragedies; how musical recitation preserved and perpetuated through centuries without the aid of manuscripts the magical fragments, some of them almost epics in length, out of Irish literature; and how the Church a thousand years ago phrased even the articles of the Creed to the appropriate rhythms of Gregorian notation. It is with the training of a classical student, therefore, that he approaches the song which is to have the accompaniment of his voice; having attended to the interpretative study, he gives his heart to the vocal rendition. Bravo, bravo! say the specialized critics to the understanding multitudes.

Happy is the poet whose lyric obtains that perfect reading. How Tennyson would have rejoiced if his "Bugle Song," which he himself delighted to read aloud, could have had McCormack's perfect reading! Alice Meynell's exquisite sonnet, "Renunciation," calls for such a reader to have ultimate perfection. What new charms attach to ordinary ballads, ordinary in both line and melody, when

The Service of the Voice

they are accorded the high privilege! Eugene Field has won richer regard for his "Little Boy Blue" than he could ever have dreamed would be its fortune; the humble hero in "The Bard of Armagh" tells his story more appealingly than when he laid down his harp in death; and "The Star Spangled Banner," which no schoolboy could ever make smooth in its halting scansions and cumbersome phrases, has at length a voice worthy of its best sentiments.

A more explicit illustration from one of his early programs will merit consideration; it will augment the proof that McCormack in his song recitals is indeed a lecturer in poetry interpretations, that he is educating great communal classes in the appreciation of ballad and lyrical poetry. It is a simple song, inviting a reading in its own right, independently of its relative value in the present employ. Lecturers in poetry may cite it among specimens done by the apostles of simplicity in diction, such as Wordsworth was; and this is a specimen, as Thomas MacDonough has said, of modern Anglo-Irish, "a language yet unspoiled by the overgrowths of literature"; and he added, "Such an Irish poet can still express himself in the simplest terms of life and of the common furniture of life." The poet here is Padraic Colum, and his manner is "the

Irish mode," surely a promising influence that the future student is to note in English literature.

The poem in question is a cradle song; and McCormack is versed in the cycle of "suantree" melodies which are inwoven in such songs. Even in a mere reading of the lines, as he does extensively in his study hour, how he delights to vocalize the dim nuances of sound, whispering, for instance, *pianissimo*, "the peering of things across the half-door."

> O men from the fields,
>   Come gently within!
> Tread softly, softly,
>   O men coming in!
>
> Mavourneen is going
>   From me and from you,
> Where Mary will fold him
>   With mantle of blue,—
>
> From reek of the smoke
>   And cold of the floor,
> And the peering of things
>   Across the half-door.
>
> O men from the fields,
>   Soft, softly come through!
> Mary puts round him
>   Her mantle of blue.

Here we have the perfect achievement: a lyrical ballad by Colum, a "suantree" melody out of

The Service of the Voice

incomparable Irish sources (the adaptation is by Harty) and the voice of McCormack. Where is a Lamartine to describe the effect? Bossuet's marvelous voice was the servant of a sublime apostleship; it proceeded from a mind and heart thinking aloud for God. And in our other instance of the service of voice we have a mind and heart thinking and feeling through the ecstatic terms of song to the delight of mankind, interpreting for multitudes the lights and shadows in thought and picture which inhabit the realms of lyric and ballad poetry.

A CLERIC'S LITERARY LABORATORIES

It would be a commonplace to remark that things upon one's own street are commonplace; that, therefore, they are rarely set into the focus of admiration; and that even under the microscope of gossip they are likely to be minimized rather than enlarged. Hearts in relationship are not wordy at their own hearths. Publicity has a psychology, whose formula is an old adage in many languages: distance lends enchantment to the view, or as Tacitus put it, *Omne ignotum pro magnifico est.* American artists, musicians for instance, after long training, go abroad for a time, thereupon to be reintroduced to America. In line with that psychology, an author and his books may dazzle his American clientèle, amaze them out of their apathy, if they wear the imprint of an English publishing house. Yet, without the halo of that moonlight, there are American writers to whom compatriotic discernment offers the laurel of esteem and a chorus of acclaim: *Agite, adplaudamus.* Glancing for immediate proof of this at our own street—it is a commonplace, Kenedy's on Barclay Street—we find

A Cleric's Literary Laboratories   135

on a goodly shelf of books the name of Francis P. Donnelly, S.J. He has the imprint of other publishers, as well as that of the Barclay Street firms; and his books have their habitats in the many longitudes and latitudes of these long and broad United States: witness the boutonniere which embellishes more than one of them—*seventh edition*.

Father Donnelly's achievement likewise contains many names in its predicate: three books appertaining to the science of literature; books four in number and four times worth while in the science of asceticism, and his volumes that belong to belles-lettres, five in prose and one in verse. To have accomplished so much and so well as a principal vocational work would be a boast, but what is to be thought of it when one realizes that this output was an avocational effect, splendid things done on the march, elaborated in fragments of time, in "the wee sma' hours" between classrooms? Quality is indissolubly wedded to his quantity; *multum* is the better half of his *multa*. If he has not been abroad, in the popular sense of the tourist, he knows a geography from many heights: from Mount Sinai and the Hills of Judea, which see farther than the horizons of natural ethics; from the Areopagus looking down on vales of Greek culture, and farther still, to classic consequences in Latin life and literature; from the Island of Saints and Scholars whose traditions are the glory of yesterdays and shall be vital in the literary destiny of tomorrows; and from Bunker Hill where the fires of patriotism still light the farthest reaches of American land and sea.

Allow his excellent treatises in the science of education to pass with mere nominal mention: *Model English* in two volumes, *The Art of Interesting*, and his practical edition of Newman's *Second Spring*. They have won an *imprimatur* from ten thousand hands, an *ex cathedra* pronouncement from the secular schools as well. In the science of pedagogy few American scholars exhibit a historical knowledge of the subject equal to his. Twenty years in the Jesuit classroom document any theory or illustration which he advances.

In the department of ascetic literature—it is literature—Father Donnelly proves that quiet oratories may be intensive laboratories. Four volumes attest a busy scriptorium. Their "pages of interest and profit," as "Aguecheek" once termed such a shelf, are for the general reader; they contain also *addita* for the clerical employ, directions for one who must be retreat-master, the corypheus to some devotional hour. They constitute a library for retreat houses; they are a retreat for any house.

Take the *Watching an Hour*. How skilfully it is woven, the three-ply cloth, its chapters done in trilogy. The loom is Ignatian, the warp is American in illustrations taken from today's closet and street, and the woof is a golden thread taken now from the Gospels or from the Fathers and Doctors of the Church, and again from secular sources as old as Plato. The captions of the chapters have the skill of a display-window to engage your attention: devotion with the gesture of rhetoric will explain the "Articles." For instance: Foxes, Dogs, Swine: our Lord called Herod a fox, He also said, "Give not that which is holy to dogs, neither cast ye your pearls before swine"; and around the text how thoughtfully the context is enlarged. Eighteen adjectives name the captions for the leading chapters in *The Heart of the Gospel*, and eighteen more for the hearts in *The Heart of Revelation*. See around that Sun of Love the planetary effulgence of Mary and Joseph, Magdalen, Peter and Paul. *Corda ad Cor loquuntur*. Expert and eloquent in Christian theology, the author is adept in the technique of structure, and he is a litterateur with stylistic investitures. May that Kingdom come: may the sacred drama of the Heart engage the amphitheaters of the world.

Coming from those oratories, regard Father

138 *Under College Towers*

Donnelly's achievement in laboratories of belles-lettres. His book on the *Art of Interesting* is proof that he has the art: the book itself is a *fait accompli*. List with it his volume of verse, *Shepherd My Thoughts*, and those charming essay books, *Mustard Seed*, and its twin, *Chaff and Wheat*.

In the fields of versification, Father Donnelly has had an interesting avocation. To hark back to the efforts of his college days at Fordham is to mention T. A. Daly, "Tom," if you please, or T. A. D., as his letters are subscribed. Solving versified charades started these young collegiate poetasters; they grew to write better riddles than they found, and now they both belong in a select catalogue of American Catholic poets. Father Donnelly took to a service which he has continued to this day: he wrote college songs then; he is now "on occasion" a contributor to the needs of a cause. As a Jesuit Scholastic his name was famous to many decades of the Woodstock Walking Club. (Ah! those cycles of song across Maryland country on every Thursday morning.) Father Donnelly was the poet laureate; listen, *cantantibus omnibus, duce Patre Frisbee:*

>   Come down ye young logicians,
>   Come down ye metaphysicians,
>   Come from chemistry,

A Cleric's Literary Laboratories 139

> Give up your mathematics,
> Come down from rooms and attics,
> Come out with W. W. C.

These playthings of other days do not appear in his book; other songs done in a spirit of service are there, in American and Irish tune and time. Yet these are not to be adduced as proof of poetic power; they are merely functional; they arose for a little hour of service, and not from an inspiration, not from such moods as produced the "Star-Spangled Banner" or the "Marseillaise" or "God Save Ireland." But his book has wheat abundant against the straws of chaff. A thinker as well as an observer, Father Donnelly finds tongues in trees, sermons in stones and good in everything, though he lack the grace of melancholy which Jacques of Shakespeare gave to his countryside. The Jesuit in his "point" sometimes displays the recondite too much, *trop recherché*. His time measures are at times too measured; the classic scansions hold him too accurately, and his lyrics are too pressed with syllabification, every note of a melody having its syllable when syncopation or the half-silences of the "slur" would have caught the heart as well as the breath. To such metrics Moore would have written (for the italics are not his) :

> 'Tis the last, last rose of the summer
> Left a-blooming now all alone.

But these observations concern externals; the verses have, like the king's daughter, a beauty within—pearls that sparkle in profound thoughtfulness, velvety cadences around the assurances of character: "Blessed are the clean of heart, for they shall see God." The thoughts, however, again have the gesture of the precise scholar rather than of ecstasy; logical rather than emotional, they rise in straight lines, and not in a mist which knows how to be roseate and warm. To advance names for a comparison he seems to be in a company with Father Tabb and Cardinal Newman. Object lessons which were theirs gather to his study. He is almost Tabb in this:

SANCTITY

> Across the soul the rays
> Of purer sunlight enter in;
> And lo! the startled gaze
> Detects the floating notes of sin.

He is nearer Newman, nearer in sound and in sense, with this:

> Let all time's saddening misbelief march out,
> Dreams of false science, brilliance of dissent,
> Unriddled facts, whatever subtleties invent
> To drive faith's weakness to the edge of rout;

A Cleric's Literary Laboratories 141

>Let loose the deadly phalanxes of doubt
>Madly to storm at every battlement,
>While all the hideous air is rent
>With jeering mockery and blatant shout.
>
>Then baffled reason seems to yield retreat;
>But should the soul chill to the touch of death
>Or bleed with some deep wound of grief,
>Tho' the dazed mind were crushed by trampling feet,
>The yearning heart would whisper with last breath,
>"Lord, I believe; help Thou my unbelief."

If verse is the higher form for one's message—who shall gainsay it?—Father Donnelly, however, speaks himself best in the prose of his little essays. Two exquisite volumes sparkle with scintillations of thought and fancy, fecund and clever. His satire is refined always; it is not steeped in pessimistic vitriol: for instance, "No weakness is found in life without some palliations to temper its unattractiveness." There is a laugh with the snap of the whip. And these essays, let us repeat, what a vogue they would have if they bore a foreign imprint! Hazlitt, albeit in a larger way, wrote such pages in a former century; and in our day one thinks of Hilaire Belloc in the comparison; and, because of a fecundity in paradox and antithesis, of Gilbert K. Chesterton.

These volumes of wheat and chaff, of little seeds from the prolific mustard seed, are surely a *vade mecum* for any five-foot shelf. In the achievement credit also the tailor who dressed them so fittingly, the publisher who knows the art of attractiveness, and he is Kenedy of Barclay Street. But the chief merit lies in the author's point of view, those horizons wherein his thought and skill operate. His lookout is higher than that of a mere scholar in Latin and Greek and in contemporaneous literature; his cosmos is larger than that of Hebrew ancients, of whom he writes in an essay on the imagination, "They began their writings on a plane infinitely above Latin or Greek or other pagans. Their horizons went beyond the farthest stars. They did not look up to but look down upon creation because they saw it through the gaze of the Creator."

Father Donnelly is an intimate house-guest in the Christian hostel; he converses with the fields where history and theology and mysticism gather flowers for the Tabernacle and its miracles, enumerating them with Lessius and calling others to watch an hour with the Heart of Revelation. To an unfailing antiphon he tunes his editorials and his meditations both in prose and verse.